DOOR OF PAPER

Essays and Memoirs

Books by Jayanta Mahapatra

Poetry

Random Descent (2006)
Bare Face (2000)
Shadow Space (1997)
The Best of Jayanta Mahapatra (1995)
A Whiteness of Bone (1992)
Temple (1989)
Burden of Waves and Fruit (1988)
Selected Poems (1987)
Dispossessed Nests (1986)
Life Signs (1983)
Relationship (1980)
The False Start (1980)
Waiting (1979)
A Rain of Rites (1976)
A Father's Hours (1976)
Svayamvara and Other Poems (1971)
Close the Sky, Ten by Ten (1971)

Poetry Translations

A Time of Rising (2003)
Discovery and Other Poems (2001)
Tapaswini (Co-translator) (1998)
Verticals of Life (1996)
I Can, But Why Should I Go? (1994)
Song of Kubja and Other Poems (1981)
Wings of the Past (1976)
Countermeasures (1973)

Prose

The Green Gardener (1997)
Orissa (1987)

DOOR OF PAPER
Essays and Memoirs

Jayanta Mahapatra

AUTHORSPRESS

Worldwide Circulation through Authorspress Global Network
First Published 2007
by
Authorspress
E-35/103, Jawahar Park
Laxmi Nagar, Delhi-110 092
e-mail: authorspress@yahoo.com

Door of Paper: Essays and Memoirs
ISBN 81-7273-374-7

Printed in India at Tarun Offset, Delhi.

In Memoriam

Frederick Morgan

(1922 - 2004)

Acknowledgements

The author and publishers wish to thank the editors of the following magazines/publications in which the essays and prose pieces in this book first appeared:

Asiaweek (Hong Kong)

The Hudson Review (New York)

The Poetry Review (New York)

The Dalhousie Review (Halifax)

The Toronto South Asian Review (Toronto)

The Times Literary Supplement (London)

Haritham (Kottayam)

Indian Horizons (New Delhi)

Indian Literature (New Delhi)

The Indian Post (Bombay)

The Literary Criterion (Mysore)

The Hindu Literary Review (Chennai)

Span (New Delhi)

The Telegraph (Calcutta)

Swagat (New Delhi)

The Times of India Review (Bombay)

The Bombay Literary Review (Bombay)

The Illustrated Weekly of India (Bombay)

Keynote (Bombay)

The Heritage (Madras)

Soviet Literature (Moscow)

World Literature Today (Norman, Oklahoma)

Contents

1

Freedom as Poetry: The Door

There is a door in the heart of man which never opens. Or if it does at times, we are not aware of its opening. When it does, it goes on to reveal another world—a world where time falls away, and space grows; perhaps the self fills with vastness and light. When one is a child, and the darkness of the world is real and tangible around him, perhaps he catches a glimpse of the opening of that door, and stares outward, blind. Lifted by an invisible gleam of light, the child is felt by it and lightened, as the instant carries him away to a place he had not known before, into a realm of freedom.

As a boy I remember one of those simple pleasures which seemed to provide me with a new beginning or give a new meaning to my days. This was when I would let my feet hang still into the waters of a flowing stream and feel the flow go past me. But it was not merely the sweep of the water which I felt then that gave me the pleasure I am speaking of now; it was something else perhaps, something I was not conscious of at that time—something that had its roots in what I wanted to do and then did without any thought of the world that stood there beside me, without being aware of the grass and the earth, and perhaps of the stars that swung on pleasantly through the skies. What do I remember now of this simple moment of the past? What is it that sticks in my mind today? Did I have the slightest idea what it might be, not knowing for sure whether I was searching for something or really trying to get away from it all?

Today, years and years later I have come to realise that this simple pleasure which could make me feel strange and sad and light at the same time was something I can call freedom. And in this 'freedom' rested the beginnings of faith, of an inexplicable lightness, which was like the spreading glow from a lamp, moving away, carrying one away as it were from everything else, something which fails to measure the expanse of one's life. For me, today, a good poem probably just does that. And a poem I might call good is one which can get down to the essence of life through the pleasure of the arbitrary coherence of the poem's words. What is remarkable is, that poetry can prove this. For true poetry does have the ability to 'liberate' both poet and reader from their necessities and produce in their minds an effect beyond the ordinary. Could we refer to this liberation or freedom that a poem can create as the poem's magic?

What is the poet's freedom? Is it the path through unknown places of the heart, a path that is both unreal and of a transcendent nature and yet is something that foresees the event of death? Is it like a moment when one hears faraway waves, falling breakers turn into some miraculous drug which can keep away the knowledge of death?

Or, for instance, is it in the lines of Kim Chi Ha, the Korean poet, when he talks of himself? I quote:

> I shouldered the weight of heart's remorse and took flight.
> As mountain ridges turned and twisted
> in that shout, that faraway city
> dawn returned at last
> in the bloodshot eyes of friends;
> through the beatings in the rusted cells,
> through that desolate freedom
> as the dew moistened my warm forehead.
>
> "A Smile" (trs. David R. McCann)

Whatever this freedom is, it cannot be denied that the process of the writing of poetry fulfils a certain inner need, which takes the poet past himself, as a part of him tries to fight the dominance of a world within him. The act of writing itself gives birth to truth, for it helps to rid oneself of things in its mysterious manner even when one has no need to be cured of our human purposes. And so, self-expression becomes one of the most important human activities, turning the poem which the poet makes into an unavoidable symbol of liberation and confinement. I say confinement because of the constraints of the words and sentences which hold the flight of the poem. Yet in spite of these, the freedom in the poem becomes a very real one, making us human and benign, and never a myth as is sometimes thought of.

Broadly speaking, one tends to feel that there are two kinds of poetry being written today, in almost all countries of the world—the one which caters more or less to the establishment, and which is relatively safe poetry because it carries no sort of risk or danger to the poet. The other, and this type of verse has been written in other times as well and in many places including our own, becomes a dangerous occupation—because, generally, such poetry is critical of the establishment and therefore is against the well-being of the poet. Here I am *not* talking of a deliberately written verse which can be labelled 'political', but of a poetry which the poet or writer should be responsible to, such a responsibility only becoming possible when the poet himself is responsible or answerable to his conscience. This is not to suggest that the poet should be taking up in some way the work of the philosopher or the man of religion—but of the poet experiencing all over again that voice from deep inside himself, and may be just doing what he has always been under the necessity to do in the many lives facing him in the world where he exists.

When I think of my own self, I feel that much of the poetry I have written has been all the time asking questions of my life so that one comes up suddenly somewhere and encounters an image of oneself one had not seen before or had merely glimpsed in some vague form sometime. Often such questionings have surfaced on the edge of answers. All this makes me realise how confused I am—a person very much like the nameless person I pass by every day in the street.

I try to understand what is happening with the poetry I write. And I suppose it would be right to assume that the same sort of process is defining poets everywhere. I look at the poem I have written, look closely into it, listen to it. And it makes a demand on me to make me ask myself: Have I written the poem for my own sake, to show to myself and to others how clever I am? Is it a mere game I have played, this poem of mine, a game with time and that absence which comes alive at the thought of death? Or is the poem there on the page, facing me because something has been *happening*?

If there is any humility left in me, in this part of me where nothing really happens, then it is time I feel I should ask myself: Am I living my life as well as a human being who feels and cares for his fellow beings? If my answer is yes, and the poems I write make sense of life, then there is evidence enough that poetry becomes freedom, and the human spirit reaches toward fulfilment.

Even though the world today is constantly in a state of flux, and things aren't what they were a decade ago, one has the feeling that very few poets are *not* responsible to the dictates of their consciences, for very few of us indeed have given up the purest of ties that exist between poetry and truth. In this unending process of writing poetry, one is always trying to recognise oneself, finding out ultimately which part of oneself will finally outcast the other part.

Poetry is the stranger within oneself—the man inside one is unaware of, and the poet is almost always in the quest of finding this other one. Therefore, his questions: Who am I? Where have I come from and where is it I am going? How should I live? How can I see that other whom I had not seen before clearly? Where are you, Other One? Have I no right to my death?

Very simple questions indeed. Yet difficult to find the appropriate answers. Only silences stare back at us, like the sound of the waves beating against the wall of the sea. Our thought is a process, the poem itself is a process—and the process holds considerable amounts of freedom and energy. And, the poet, in his poetry, is trying to find something that will endure behind the many masks he encounters—in himself most of all perhaps—maybe something that would in the end help to clarify his vision, and which he does through the very act of his writing.

So the freedom and energy in poetry, and the consequent healing that takes place as one goes on to discover and rediscover the many things connected with one's life. Let us admit this quality of mystery that poetry holds in its making.

Sometimes, for hours together I sit through the night, watching despair—this blank sheet of paper in front of me. I experience the fearful pull of gravity which pulls me down when words fail to appear on the paper. Then, suddenly maybe, the language is there, flowing into rhythm, like the unseen wind moving the branches of the mango tree in my little courtyard. There is a flow of energy as the poem builds up, building up too the feeling of weightlessness, a sort of zero gravity one can call freedom.

Towards the end of this piece, I ask myself: What am I made of? Of hunger and earth and homesickness? Yet I realise I cannot help being affected by the world around me, by a sensitivity to issues that plague my country and the world today. And in order to understand who I am and who I will become, I shall go on writing my poems as the sun goes on shining—both on the carefully-tended roses in the President's vast gardens and on the rat-riddled shacks in my town where starving children pray to God. And weary, perhaps abandoned, surrounded by my own words which crowd me down, I try to escape, thinking of another kind of freedom.

Who will cry the cry of the dropping leaf? Who will whisper the whisper of the summer breeze? The politician or the poet?

Perhaps poetry shall always remain an attempt to remove the burden of time from this world, and poems will continue to be written, through images, metaphors, symbols. Time, ever present, ever passing, making us wakeful while we are asleep, making us hear our pulse in the silence of the night. I quote a line from the *Atharva Veda* XIX: 53.

Time drives as a horse with seven reigns, thousand-eyed, unageing, possessing much seed; him the inspired poets mount; his wheels are all beings.

And one asks: Does a poet use time to get away from time? Does he surrender to this rite, capturing on time a fragile moment of meaning? Merely for the sake of the feeling of freedom?

Again and again, one returns from that closed door. Someone is there, standing over the shoulder. I don't know what the one standing there wants. What, however, is amazing to me is that I can write a poem through my anguish and the awareness of my presence and in the process reveal myself—perhaps going out of myself, leaping into blindness or light. Call it *freedom*. For what we dream can well enter the realm of undream, causing something to come out of it, something like a quiet self-discovery or even prayer, that brings a joy in the recognition of ourselves against the fear of time. Call it *freedom*.

So maybe the need to be human is important in a poet than in anyone else, worse in a poet because a poet's business is to see—which he should do, listening to the voice of his inner self. Let the poet not bother about the conscience of the world—simply *be* the water that flows, finding its own level, even if it is soaked away by the earth, with no trace left behind. In this, in such a poetry of today, committed to the many worlds we live and believe in—the human, the historical and the moral—can one touch the heart of freedom.

Will poetry, therefore, give some sort of meaning to the substance of life, to reality, touching it with freedom? Or, is it freedom that will give poetry its reality—its ability to speak of the importance of man?

2

An Orissa Journal: July to November

If you happen to be anybody trying to prise open the skin of this land of myth and antiquity, to discover the roots of the excitement that seems to run through all the primitive commonplace responses evident around you, it is certain you will not find anything. A kind of struggle floats in the air and laps the hearts of men: the struggle just to live, against drought and flood, storm and fever. Nothing more. They wear no masks. They are simply people who believe that things happen as they do because they happen as the consequence of things that have happened before, and that nothing can change the sequence of things. And so they can suffer one day after the other, for a whole lifetime, while the sun and rain wash them. There are truths one senses here, like hunger or the need to be lazy, or the worship of an ancestor.

Punctuated with fairs and festivals, feasts and fasting, life, for most of the inhabitants, insinuates itself into a deeper inner world of ancient mysterious symbols, visual and auditory. The capacity to recognise the rooted underground traditions of their ancestors, even in the face of a new changing reality, and to derive peace or perhaps a state of stupefied happiness, is a haunting quality difficult to find elsewhere. Rationalist as I am, it puzzles me, puts me in doubt. It is a vision, one presumes, that can emanate from faith, a vision one has to learn to encounter. A vision which begins with a word: *Shanti*, the word of peace, in a pursuit of life's meaning. Here life is lived in an endlessly recurring cycle, as it has been through hundreds of years.

The town of Cuttack lies on a gently undulating plain. Two rivers encircle the town, and all roads lead to one or the other. Ruins have piled up through the years. A small fort still stands somewhat defiantly, surrounded by a shallow moat. One comes across places where guns had been mounted, the old stone balustrades, dark granaries looking like inverted bowls—these are trophies of the wars that the local soldiers fought against the British. There are the narrow, nicked lanes full of turns, so easy to lose your way in. This is the real India: gentle roads hanging in the red dust, the men padding along in their billowy *dhoties*, basking in the sun, smoking, gossiping. Walking the twisted streets on early mornings, I seem to hear the clack of wooden clogs behind me on the worn-out stones, and the rhythm of *mantras* chanted by bearded sages in flowing ochre robes. By the doors of close-packed dwellings, behind the broken facades, are hints of the music of silver anklets moving across the inner courtyards, while in the eyes of women walking to the river for their daily bath lingers the promise of mysteries too ancient for me to understand.

Today, as I write this, a cyclone has hit the jagged Orissa coastline and gone. It has become a regular feature, these cyclonic storms coming in from deep inside the Bay of Bengal, the familiar weather bulletins from the Calcutta station of All India Radio: A depression has occurred in the Bay, and was centred at 8.30 a.m. Indian Standard Time at a point 550 kilometres east-south-east of Puri, etc.... Once again, someone beside me says. The day wearily moves on, the next forty-eight hours become thirty-six. People of the low-lying areas along the coast are evacuated to safer places. In the villages children are not allowed to go to school. The elders reach for their coarse, musty blankets. The thatched roofs of most houses have already been made secure with strong ropes of straw. Far away the wind is young and new at first, as I strain my ears for its coming. The air gradually turns ominous. In a few minutes the postcard sky vibrates with the stampeding of a thousand jungle elephants.

Stubbornly the rain and wind lash the countryside. A taste of charcoal stays in the mouth. I look out cautiously at times through the window. There is the fierce rain. I turn on my battery-operated radio, hear the meteorological reports again and again, let these run through me and surround me with a mood of participation. Only the bubble-eyed gecko behind the picture frame on the wall goes on tut-tutting like an evil omen.

And so the storm continues. I lie in my warm bed. Two days have brought me certain small discomforts and disappointments like power failure and no water. That is all. The Delhi and Calcutta newspapers have not arrived. A hundred miles up north, a few yards of railway track have been washed away. I watch for news of the outside world. And when I hold my wife's hand in the darkness, a firefly spreads its blue flower of flame and stills the silence in my mind. And as usual with many people, I am unaware of what has happened around me, firmly ensconced in my own five senses, in an easy, snug, sheltered world.

When dawn comes, it is not like the night before. I wake early, still sleepy. The stupid crickets have fallen silent. White clouds have slipped quietly in through the dark, moving fast, loosening, moving west in the wind. Memories seem to flit like clouds in the sky. I listen. There is the sharp clatter of boys in the road searching for the night's gleaming jasmines to carry away for the morning *puja*. I open my stale mouth wide and inhale a full breath of the freshened air. Some stray mosquitoes hover around my body, stinging me. These have not yet found the new shadows of the morning's light; I try to slap one, miss it, follow it with my eyes as it dips into the dark interior of a bookcase. In the ugly, squat, cage-like building across the road, the lights are suddenly switched on. The women of the household are probably awake. A crow zips past in the half light, perches on the parapet of the house and starts to caw lustily. I see the woman then, her round succulent face showing through her gauzy cotton wrap, walk up to the parapet and shoo the crow away. She notices me, pulls the wrap closer so as to conceal her face, turns and hustles inside, in a gesture of apparent disdain.

I try to understand. Two things in the main have irritated the woman. First, she has seen me, with my stranger's face first thing in the morning, and therefore she is not sure what the day has in store for her, if my face would bring her luck. Second, she is agitated at the thought of a man staring at her. But of course there may be more than that, I do not know. Myth and superstition seem to affect our women more, disturb their unstable equilibrium of happiness. I suppose my sense of humour should let me smile. I fill my eyes with the day's warm, adolescent light. Round the bend of the road Lakshmi appears, walking purposefully, the wide-mouthed excreta bin resting like an infant across her slender left hip. Lakshmi, the fourteen-year-old outcaste sweeper girl, barefoot and smiling, cradling the faeces of the upper class with her left arm, while her right swings in unison with her small, tight, lotus-bud breasts. Oh Lakshmi, I think. By this time next year you'll be married, your peasant body will have changed, and youth will be a heavy feeling deep down under you, a lake that would only show the weak, dispersed blooms of sunlight in the water of your memory. And perhaps the fourteen years you leave behind you will be there for people like me, and for the tubercular college student living down the road who watches you every day, many empty shadows of his hands on his open book, almost like an awe.

While I am looking around, the sun has come up. Crows flying in and out, into more crows. A black, humped bull idly winds his way from the middle of the road where he has spent the late hours of night. The street hydrant in the corner gurgles as the water spirals down. Women are already heading towards it, empty pitchers on their heads. A Jain temple in the distance goes into business. I hear the ringing of brass bells that excite and sustain the human spirit. And the ragpicker woman, scrawny and old, is shuffling along, poking into the rubble heaps, taking refuge in the shadows of a faith she does not need to understand. In a sort of slow motion, the new day preoccupies in the old.

The ordinary person here takes life as it comes. Pathetic, maybe, to an outsider. Or, a sense of Indian backwardness which hits the tourist, both in the environment and in the minds of the people themselves. But that is how they have lived for a long, unchanging time—basically a simple, agricultural community. Step outside the town limits, and the fields stretch away on either side, green and rich, checkered rectangles and squares which limit their frightfully honest possessions of land. The country surrounds them like an old, intimate phenomenon. Their stability is evident. And perhaps they have stuck to their own ways because, on the whole, they have preferred them, adverse to change and the substance of the new. Each time I am here I feel the soft flutter of the earth, the sensation like the physical touch of a feminine hand in mine. More like the beginning of some mystical rite. A woman bends down in the muddy ankle-deep water in the fields, weeding, along with her husband. Perhaps she is in her eighth month with child. Only a slight swelling shows under the graceful folds of her *sari*, the ends tucked along her waist. After the day's work, she will go back and light the oil lamp in the rural twilight, and with pious rapture pray for her husband and the unborn one stirring inside her belly in front of the sacred basil in the small dung-washed courtyard.

Like the oil lamp, the ancient, pitted land sputters. I keep watch thinking it will go out, but nothing happens. The days go on, in patient sombre devotion, and with them the seasons of light and darkness, of scorching heat and unending rain. The papers report the deaths in the recent cyclone, the destruction by the twelve-foot tidal wave which swept up the coastal areas. It is difficult for me to believe the number dead, everything seems so colourless and distant from where I live. The pictures too, being published gradually in the dailies: an old man sobbing beside his dead wife and child, the naked bodies decomposed. The thought of death troubles me. It has a different perspective now. My friend Deba, who teaches in the local college, rushes in, talks of relief operations in conjuction with the YMCA. I am confused. Maybe I should accompany him and work in the stricken areas. Our talk veers toward incarnation. My experience is insoluble. And thus to the ultimate conclusion, that all those who died suddenly (the 10,000 or more) in the recent cyclone reaped the consequence for what each had done in his or her previous incarnation. My fingers behave like exposed bones. One feels suspended between *nirvana* and the laws of loosening life. And one can only sit down to write a poem at midnight, a sorry song of cause and effect.

Through the days of long sick rain, and the October sun is warm purple on my face. The air is free of dust, wine to the nose. Now is the time of worship when the skies are clear and the wagtails are back again, the tall white grasses silvering the banks of the irrigation canals. In about a week the new moon should appear, heralding the festival of *Durga Puja,* and I can feel instinctive quiverings in the air, trying to shape syllables of uninhibited laughter. Even the crows are wilder than before, the streets look bold and spectacular, and break with smiles. A light spreads slowly across the golden thatches of houses, over the slate-grey roofs of buildings, but a different autumn light, magical and serene. Every morning, at this time, I observe Govinda Maharana, the image-maker, as he walks down the road to the club-house in our locality to fashion his Durga image. I search for the familiar smile on his features, but I seem to miss it this year. Is it the terrible loss of life in the cyclone which affects him? Perhaps the death of a sister or brother, I do not know. I can picture him gazing intently at his work, his critical eyes moving around from one point to another of the clay image, the tender muscles, the mouth, the ten arms, the many fingers he has created with passion; and I discover at last the humility of a human who realises that he has to shape the likeness of his supreme goddess, Durga, in the dual role of creator and destroyer.

The new moon appears, a faint arc of light, for only an hour in the evening sky. Govinda has begun the enamelling of his image. Easily the colours flow onto the bare, chalked body of the goddess—vivid greens and vermilion and haunting shades of peacock blue—while from time to time he jets aside a blob of spittle from the *pan* leaf he chews in his mouth. I walk down to the club-house, peep through the chink in the wide tarpaulins he has hung at the entrance to keep his work hidden from passers-by. He sees me, we exchange greetings. He is working carefully at the eyes, deep and large and gentle, like those of a cow. I feel his work tentatively. Like his father before him, and his father's father, Govinda stolidly pursues his ancient craft, and I cannot but notice a certain inner impulse which drives him on, part poetic, part divine.

For five days, the world is high. People are out in the open streets of the town, diverse groups, clustered like ants around the gaily decorated images of gods and goddesses. And among them, pushing, jostling, are the beggars, seemingly everywhere. Lepers in red cotton caps, their faces lumpy, leonine—feet wrapped in soiled bandages, shuffling along, cans hanging from multilated hands. At times someone loses patience and tries to ward them off with angry shouts, but invariably they take no notice and press forward into the crowd, spitting out venomous abuse. All the while the festivities continue, drums and cymbals shatter the air, and heads of devotees keep on bowing before the deities. It is not only that the goddess Durga is worshipped, but Siva too, and his consort, Parvati. One is struck by the superb artistic vision of these simple clay modellers, and is reminded of the numerous sculptures that form the friezes and panels of Orissan temples. It becomes apparent that the male and female images are a manifestation of the duality desired by the supreme God: they represent the earthly symbols of procreation. One of the *Upanishads* says:

> The woman is the fire,
>   her womb the fuel,
> the invitation of a man
>   the smoke.
> The door is the flame,
>   the entering the ember,
>   pleasure the spark.
> In this fire the gods form
>   the offering.
> From this offering springs forth
>   the child.

I look up at the images. A gentle light flickers on ivory cheeks, shadowed serene eyes, making them alive. For a moment I forget myself. Something floats down to earth as I stand there, from the constellations beyond, and breathes with the breath of incense spilling into the night where the crowds are, moulded into a viscous human mass, everywhere. I hold my breath. The giant temple drums rumble on. The physical perspective changes every moment; perhaps this is what hammers on the shell of one's inherent isolation, that time is not constant, and the present is not the present any longer. Slowly I realise that I am living at one particular instant in many layers of time—the mythic, the historical and the present. What one sees in the present is only what has stirred the air of the place for countless generations.

One festival follows another. Otherwise the days move in the same, placid, nothing-whatever manner. A slight nip in the air, and the urban upper-class women are to be seen more often in their gardens, directing their gardeners to plant the winter seasonals in well-arranged beds. I can see my neighbour, Mrs. Sen, from my window, her hair tied up in an exciting, perky ball, about six inches in diameter. One of the latest fads from Bombay, which resembles a rounded boulder precariously perched on another. I wonder at the ease with which she moves about. Erect, proud in her bearing, her thirty-five years look like twenty-one. Lakshmi comes to my mind; perhaps youth lasts a year for her, no more. And the Mrs Sen types, flaunting the knowledge of the three K's—the Kamasutra, Konarka, and Khajuraho—in their affluent living rooms, seem a sorry feedback of sex from the west.

On a Sunday I decide to take the early morning bus out of town. Winter is a happy time, the Puri sea is calm, and this temple town is a mere fifty miles away. The bus is already stuffed with passengers by the time I enter and find a seat in the rear. The roads are almost deserted at this hour. Small heaps of coal burn desolately in iron stoves by the roadside: the cheap tea-places are beginning to open. We move up to the highway. There are the village women sitting on their haunches in the paddy fields, at the call of nature, easing themselves—quite a familiar sight at dawn and dusk. Village houses have no lavatories, everyone uses the open, it is more hygienic. Two shy girls stand up when our bus passes by: smiling, one covers her face while the other turns around and looks the other way. I can hear the barbets calling from the bushes. My bus appears to have a limitless capacity; more and more people push their way in at every stop. At the railway level crossing we stop for a passing express. A stubbed hand is jabbed into my face, fortunately coming to an abrupt halt about ten inches from my right eye.

I turn my face away, pretending not to notice the crippled lepers begging around the bus. Some young woman in one of the front seats drops a coin into the outstretched palm, compassion oozing from her features. The beggar coolly proceeds ahead, he sees no reason to be grateful. Maybe this is the way, I tell myself, when the donor would move her soul, slowly but surely, through the long process of reincarnation, and free herself from the sins of the flesh to achieve her longed-for sainthood.

It takes a long four-and-a-half hours to reach Puri. A good distance from the town limits, the spire of the great temple of Jagannath comes into view. The customary folding of hands, heads bowing again. Mistily, I observe the clusters of coconut palms afloat in the warm, humid air. A lone lammergeyer circling high above. The bus swerves sharply, stops for a line of loaded bullock carts lumbering out of the town. We crawl through a constricted village road, flanked by thatched mud huts slanting down at an angle, their front doors wide open. Striking designs done in white chalk paint stand out on the ochre walls: sacred emblems made for the purpose of living rather than for beauty or display. These drawings are conventional folk symbols used by the womenfolk to flatter their gods—particularly on festive occasions; again a dramatisation of their religious belief.

I look at the time. It is ten o'clock. At the outskirts of the village we pass through, the pond lies in the sun, its face a speckled green, ringed by palms and a clump of bamboo at the water's edge, thin long leaves littering the surface. Lean brown men throng the stagnant water like flies around the flat flagstones, as the day's heat whirrs beyond the water's dark interior. Each little leisurely movement of the morning bath becomes part of a ritual, bears a pious significance, as I visualise the lips of the bathers moving effortlessly and yet ceremoniously to some old weatherproof prayer. And I see the naked, starry-eyed children staring up at me, smiling with their swollen bellies, and I recollect their rationed youth; yet it does not seem to matter to them, their calm, inexorable innocence accusing me while I go searching in a frantic world.

Puri opens like a maw in the mind. You seem somewhat afraid to be there, yet one time or another something drags you there without your knowing. All the time you feel its huge heart pounding on, beyond you, in the immediate darkness—not beating for its own, but for those millions who come here every year, once at least before their present lives end. My bus bumps unevenly over the one giant main street that leads straight to the Great Temple. Its immensity is surprisingly tender; I experience the touch of a huge hand beneath me, through my skin. I cannot explain it. That autumn when I was five I had strayed from my father's side, lost in the milling crowds near the temple. Three hours later, I was found playing unconcerned and happy in the courtyard of a saffron-robed, bearded ascetic. Yet for all this, the town teems with thieves, beggars and touts, especially at the time of the centuries-old car festival. On this holy day, the Lord Jagannath mounts his famous forty-five-foot high wooden chariot, and along with his elder brother, Balabhadra, and their sister, Subhadra, make their symbolic tour of the universe, the three heavy chariots pulled clumsily with long thick ropes by sweating, hysterical devotees on the one-and-a-half-mile journey. Thus, every year, when the monsoon sets, the Lord of the universe performs his tour of the world to study the state of mankind.

Besides this major festival, there are no fewer than sixty-one other festivals for the gods. It is a place of opportunity for priests and the local people to make easy money off the flocking pilgrims who seem to walk in circles around the ache of their apparently empty existence.

It is six p.m. when I push past the rows of lighted stalls glittering with sea shells, beads, bangles, and soft stone carvings, and walk towards the temple entrance. The garrulous sparrows have settled down for the night. The cool sea breeze cannot find its way in here. I feel warm. The massive doors are open. A priest hurries towards me, smiling, mumbles something about offering atonement, rattles off the names of my ancestors to impress me. I say no, I don't need any help, take my shoes off and enter the precinct, barefoot. There is a thick crowd inside, motley, sad; mostly white-clad widowed women, children, and the always-present old. The place is well lighted. The marble flagstones under my feet are inscribed with the names of their donors. The sweet aroma of incense and flowers overpowers me. I walk up a flight of steps, then down until I reach the damp inner sanctum characteristic of any Hindu place of worship. Convention, the swaying darkness, a fable. I am not allowed to proceed further. Ten feet away, three gods, dark, dark and strange, limbless, grotesque—and I am here. Stark eyes, white, unblinking, gazing into my abyss. I can feel my fingers curl into my palms. A priest taps my head hard with his flat, holy stick, shouts at me to move on. The *darshana* is over. The hot, pushing crowd submerges me. I cannot breathe. From the corner of my eye I notice a man press forward against a pretty young bride, then clumsily crumple one heavy round breast with his hand, and vanish swiftly in the crowd. Every time, I tell myself, every time, but this is neither a silence nor an answer. Obviously I have missed something. I remember the first rain, the precious wet clods of earth, the remnants of a lost childhood—and now this circuit before me with thoughts like nimbuses tumbling across. Is this the infinity I have not been able to fathom?

When I come out of the temple, I seem to hear the doors crash behind. I look back. A crowd is out there. A world. Perhaps I would like to be with *them*. Within and without. A hippie couple, strolling towards the gates, hand-in-hand, mouths partly open. I hear the hawk cuckoo's cry, haunting and mysterious, racing through the sky, a cry of passed time. I turn and look at the crowds again. And I am reminded of a huge holy flower swaying in the wind of other, greater reasons.

3

About "Hunger" and Myself

It was hard to believe the flesh was heavy on my back.
The fisherman said: will you have her, carelessly,
trailing his nets and his nerves, as though his words
sanctified the purpose with which he faced himself.
I saw his white bone thrash his eyes.

I followed him across the sprawling sands,
my mind thumping in the flesh's sling.
Hope lay perhaps in burning the house I lived in.
Silence gripped my sleeves; his body clawed
at the froth his old nets had dragged up from the seas.

In the flickering dark his lean-to opened like a wound.
The wind was I, and the days and nights before.
Palm fronds scratched my skin. Inside the shack
an oil lamp splayed the hours bunched to those walls.
Over and over the sticky soot crossed the space of my
mind.

I heard him say: my daughter, she's just turned fifteen...
Feel her. I'll be back soon, your bus leaves at nine.
The sky fell on me, and a father's exhausted wile.
Long and lean, her years were cold as rubber.
She opened her wormy legs wide. I felt the hunger there,
the other one, the fish slithering, turning inside.

To pick out a poem from among other similar poems one has written and to call it 'significant' is not an easy thing to do. Especially for someone like myself: I, who have had very little acquaintance with poetry, having studied Physics and Mathematics throughout; and then, too, having begun writing poetry late in life, rather very late.

But those, my early attempts at poems, thrilled me as nothing had ever done before. Clumsy makings perhaps, they helped me to set myself in a specific direction—I know I was beginning to turn north like a slowly magnetised lump of iron—simultaneously I also realised how weak was this field of force which propelled me to write. Even today I have to ruefully admit that poems come to me the hard way. They have always been so; and it makes me ask myself: Why is it that I can't write poems more easily? Does it point to the existence in me of a certain failing, connected to my own nature? And will I never be able to get over it?

Whatever that is, it is true. I look up with awe at a poet, when I meet one; as I did in 1976, when I came face to face with Robert Bly and Shiraishi Kazuko and Stephen Spender at the International Writing Program in Iowa City. As I did, when I met with A.D. Hope, Margaret Atwood, Galway Kinnell and Sapardi Djoko Damono at the Adelaide Festival of the Arts. And there have been other meetings....

Perhaps I might call this a 'significant' poem, significant to me because of the theme of the poem. Readers have pointed to its 'integrated form' which is generally absent from most of my poems, and they have liked the way the poem appears on the page as a finished product. I should like to emphasize the experience held in those lines, of the truth that is contained in the poem; a truth that could perhaps overflow the boundaries of the poem because of the language made in the poem. Certainly language is the medium of poetry, but language *plus* makes a good poem, and no one can deny that. I believe I have been able to make use of language in "Hunger" using the images to affirm and control at the same time the sexual drive of the protagonist.

But leaving aside the use of language in "Hunger," the poem becomes a source of sustenance to me, because of its basic human sequence, its quiet conviction. The poem is based on a true incident; it could easily have happened to me on the poverty-ridden sands of Gopalpur-on-Sea. Often have I imagined myself walking those sands, my solitude and my inherent sexuality working on me, to face the girl inside the dimly-lit, palm-frond shack. The landscape of Gopalpur chose me, and my poem. To face perhaps my inner self, to see my own debasement, to realise my utter helplessness against the stubborn starvation light of my country.

4

Mystery as Mantra

I

Mystery has always fascinated me—a sense of the unknown, of things unexplainable, even in those areas which appear so very familiar in our lives. And so it is with poetry. All poetry that touches, arousing a tremor in the heart, should have this element of the unknown in it: a manner of silence which suddenly stops the reader, as it were, expanding the horizon in which the reader finds himself. This is a type of poetry which does not appear to have attracted many readers in our country, although, judging from the traditionally built-in sense of mysticism an Indian has, such poetry should have a wide practice and readership here.

Mystery is like the rain, falling like false jewels in the sky, which catch the light as they fall, maybe like the trail of a rainbow; and perhaps it is these bits of a rainbow which a poem should catch to be able to move the reader and instil in his or her mind an alien "stirring" of some kind.

I could call this stirring in the mind a madness, which may border on irrationality; but it is exactly this quality of the unknown and un-understandable which goes to make the beauty of a poem. And this is how I feel: that one must somehow try to reach the border between things understandable and un-understandable in a poem, between life and death, between a straight line and a circle.

Perhaps this paucity of our knowledge about death, about the nowhere which exists in the mind about the knowledge of death and our future, and about this boundary when flesh goes and time enters, holds an unusual power that drives one to create the flow of a poem. And so, this unknown, the mysterious which one can never fully fathom, leads to an unending questioning in my own poetry.

Plainly speaking, it is hard to say what unknown forms of a transcendent nature poetry persists in trying to find. We have only a dim sense of the presence of such unknown forms, something akin to enormous galaxies or interstellar space through which we pass, and about which we can only imagine. And yet, although these shadowy shapes are things of conjecture, they force us down by their weight, probably becoming real and clear as matter we have been accustomed to know.

In a poem I wrote thirty years ago, titled "A Rain of Rites", I found myself once again at the border between two separate regions of the mind—between what perhaps I understood and what I did not, using "rain" as a symbol for that substance which makes up my life, those blurs of vague light that pulsate with the days, making me ask at the end of the poem, "What still stale air sits on an angel's wings? / What holds my rain so it's hard to overcome?" I suppose such questionings come from somewhere deep within oneself, and that there is no reason or rationale for these things. But such questions and such searching move me, and I am unable to resist them in my poetry. For poetry is voice—*vaak*—and it is a voice which is forged from those elements that constitute the world both within and without, a voice which carries with it its unusual power of survival.

So poetry, poetry that is Indian in essence, does take us beyond ourselves, bringing us face to face with that self on the other side, revealing suddenly the mirror opposite of the idea that has gone to make the poem. Once again, this is a coming together of opposites: like, for instance, good and evil, which can only carry themselves as ideas or exist because one has meaning only in relation to the other. One could go on citing examples from the domain of science, to show that such existence is a reality in the world of subatomic particles—the electron which has its opposite in the positron, for example—and such pairs of eternal antipodes in the minutest forms of matter. And so, one may ask, why not with poetry? If an idea is there, it must exist as a pair of opposites; if you have one, you must have the other, because one has meaning only in relation to the other. And the human mind can only think in terms of these possibilities.

But it is silence that one is faced with, after a period of writing—a silence which seems to save, to redeem. Its destruction is, to me, as perhaps to everyone else, a matter of concern. Silence is a word which comes back over and over again into my life, and, consequently, to the poetry I write. And silence exerts an air of mystery that makes me reach into the unknown, to sense things I had never felt before.

So, for me, a poem is knit together by an inconceivable silence. Silence which is an intangible substance of which words are but manifestations; words which can build the poem from a silence and to which the poem must eventually return. Does this silence lie within the heart? Maybe it does, as it waits to burst out of one with a childlike pang of pain on its way to becoming the language of a poem. For this silence is simply what the word means, nothing else. No poetic symbol. And I seem to feel it like an armour I sheathe myself in, to protect myself from the outside world.

And perhaps, at times, not having understood this silence I experience within, I let it open out for me a thousand memories, a thousand longings, as these, in turn, come into being in a poem I write. Because there is no doubt that a poem is always made in the field of one's imagination. And as I go on to write, perhaps I use this silence as a myth, and use different symbols and metaphors as they suit my own experience.

When one writes in this way, poetry enters the realm of dream, consequently making the meaning of the poem unclear. This is what some readers and critics have said about my poetry—that it tends to be obscure, not giving up its meaning easily to the reader after a reading. But I ask myself: what use is a poem if it is easily understood, if there is a straightforward working of the words of the poem, more in the manner of a statement? True poetry, perhaps, has always lent itself to an indirect approach, and where one wants to return to an overwhelming silence. It becomes difficult to explain such processes taking place in the mind.

So, because the poem happens in the mind, the poem itself becomes the idea. When I write a poem around the idea of silence, then perhaps the whole poem is my silence, not the language which clothes the idea and which might not be apparent at all to the reader of the poem.

Writing this, I realise it becomes harder and harder to explain the idea of silence and its mystery. I have measured this silence of mind with symbols like "rain" or "sleep" or "stone"—which are, once again, very private symbols. Born as we are to fundamental thoughts of doubt and uncertainty, it is not easy to predict anything in this world we live in, least of all the outcome of a poem. But the workings in the mind go on, even as I realise that the fact of observation of an object is uncertain, because it is linked with the passage of time and with the fact that we are always moving, as pointed out so aptly by Heisenberg. So also, I know of nothing for certain in this world.

The pattern of understanding has not basically changed with the poems I have written, and it will probably always be so. My themes have changed; but the poem itself, the process which goes to make the poem, will ever remain a mystery. All knowledge is provisional, so why should a poem be otherwise?

The mind in one's being is shaped by all one sees and all one has failed to see. From this mind, the poem. Once it is done, I can feel something stir in me, perhaps in a manner of consolation for things I have not been able to do. Perhaps it brings me back to reality; a curious mixture of pain and satisfaction churns my mind. It is difficult to say.

And yet, our sense of what a poem *is,* is formed out of the very fact of assimilation of those many poems we have encountered through the years, and it is no use denying that these connections have not been made in one's poetry. I should like to think that it has happened in the poetry I have written. If the quality of mystery appeals to me, then this has come from the value I have learned to place on how such language and ideas have tended to become poetry. And this poetry, like all other art, alternates between deception and revelation.

At times critics have not been nice about my poetry, because of the way I juxtapose images and symbols in my work. I guess the reader has sometimes to exert himself to find meanings from the bonds between them. One cannot deny that such poetry is mysterious, touching the abstract at times. Whether such poetry fails or succeeds is a different matter. Any judgement is one of preference, a preference influenced by education, upbringing, attitudes, and opinions often having little to do with art or aesthetics. And often these beliefs are irrationally based on social and economic factors which are determined by chance or chosen by the reader himself as profitable to his career.

Ruled by the unconscious, one is urged to come out with the mysterious in a poem. I am not insisting that this unconscious is some sort of a god or a computer gone haywire. But the self is wrapped up in too many ambiguities for comfort. And it dictates. It makes me imagine. It creates in me a wonderful need. It makes me speak in different ways to satisfy the need to say what I know and feel. And that is all I can truthfully say.

II

Of the hundreds of poetry collections that have appeared and served the Indian reading public in the last fifty years, hardly more than fifty can be taken serious note of. I mention fifty years because India gained her independence in 1947; and we could, safely, associate literary movements in poetry and fiction with the easing of tensions and a feeling of freedom that has prevailed around the country since that time. The post-Independence climate was greatly helpful in nurturing a new generation of writers, writers who believed themselves to be free to use their own regional languages to put forward the intimate credos and illusions with which they lived. Whether the results produced by these writers turned out to be serious literature is debatable; nevertheless, we look upon such attempts, which tended toward the confessional and symbolic, as attempts furthering the intellectual air of the land.

It has always appeared difficult for anyone to come to terms with the Indian poetry scene. The vastness of the subcontinent, with its varied regions, the differences in the peoples with their separate languages, often belie the suggestion made in almost all circles that the many literary movements cohere in a single Indian vision. Even a very generalised study of the writings in the twenty-plus regional languages reveals the fallacy of this opinion.

To my mind, the subdivision of the country into a number of linguistic regions undeniably goaded writers to pursue their feelings in their respective languages; and by the seventies a considerable growth in writing was evident. Creative writing became a major preoccupation. With the establishment of the Sahitya Akademi or National Academy of Letters, which, by awarding yearly prizes, accorded much-needed recognition to writing done in the various Indian languages, a new era was established. And perhaps the improved status granted to men of letters by the general public was a pleasing change. Poets and writers did seem to be more talked about, although the usefulness of such writing in a society still plagued by hunger and corruption remains a doubtful issue. It was not that there was a demand for reading matter of every kind, but the emphasis on freedom of expression encouraged by the new government gave men of letters a fairly privileged place in the aspirations of the community. Truly speaking, even today, there is no broad popular demand for original writing, and the bulk of poetry produced in the years after independence has been little more than an application of old attitudes and well-proven techniques to a new source of material that arose from the modern era's greater frankness and more confessional tendencies (particularly in matters of love and sex), no longer restricted by missionary or moral censorship.

With a strong oral tradition, from as long ago as one can remember, sages and wandering mendicants have sung episodes from the ancient epics, particularly the *Ramayana* and the *Mahabharata,* in differing versions, and this singing has been endowed with religious significance. These two epics are legends of war, circumscribed in colourful ritual. The *Mahabharata* remains the longest single poem among the literatures of the world, containing more than 90,000 stanzas. It was composed by the sage Vyasa. Therefore one of the common denominators of Indian literature as a whole has been Hindu mythology, in which ideas and content from these epics and from the *Upanishads* have been assimilated, to be used by writers right up to the present. And along with this mythological dimension, which is a powerful feeding ground for regional literatures, is the contribution of a folklore throbbingly alive in rural life. This folklore has apparently two main sources: myths and legends (the primary one), and the celebratory festive song. And strangely, the Siva/Parvati, Radha/Krishna, and Rama/Sita themes persist to hold their place even amid the fast-changing social situation in the country.

If we consider Indian literature as one, with a single literary sensibility, we could go on to classify it into three broad periods, based on chronology. The first period could cover everything up to the middle of the nineteenth century, when the English language arrived; the second would extend to approximately the middle of the twentieth century; and the last would encompass post-Independence writing from 1947. Sanskrit, our oldest language, was the medium of the *Vedas* and other epics. Related to most European languages, it was the root language from which our regional languages took form. Gradually, however, Sanskrit lost its hold on the masses, as did the cohesiveness of Hinduism, which petered out in mere ritual. Indian aesthetics disappeared, and Sanskrit died, restricted as it was to a supposedly intelligent but closed minority.

It would not be wrong to suggest that the British occupation of India slowly but surely led to a new unity among the different regions and also gave new blood to an almost stagnant literary scene. English brought with it new ideas and forms and became a major source of literary power. Indian writing during this period, i.e., from the mid-nineteenth century till the mid-twentieth, exhibits a sort of coherence that had been absent for many years. And English began to serve as a creative medium for many Indians, especially for those who lived in cities or were exposed to the British presence.

Still, it was actually with the departure of the British from India that a new seriousness in the intentions of poets and novelists writing in English became evident. One would have thought that the English language would soon be obliterated from the subcontinent, because of the antagonism toward all things British; but strangely, this did not happen. Simultaneously too, there was more writing being done in all the regional languages, and the unpretentious voice of the poet began to be heard. Not only was there an introspection, a revision of values in this new writing, but a new sincerity, frank and self-indulgent, became evident.

Surprisingly, no work of great magnitude or vision appears in any of the regional languages in continuation of the literary traditions we Indians seem to be so proud of. Somehow the Hindu view of life which had infused such vigour and subtlety into earlier writing began to wane. Only a set of formal patterns remained in use, which the regional literatures appeared to take up and elaborate. Could this casual indifference to serious literary pursuits be taken as the result of the colonisation to which the Indian people were subjected? Or did the defeats they suffered time after time leave them mere victims of an impotent nostalgia?

It was in the sixties that poetry in the regional languages began to change. The poem seemed new now, almost brutal in its nakedness—and this happened not only here in Orissa, where I live, but elsewhere as well, from Maharashtra in the west to states like Karnataka and Kerala in the south. And once again, a curious fact emerges when one studies the writing around India. These significant writers who wrote in the many regional languages were mostly English-educated academics; in other words, they were writers who had Master's degrees in English and American literature and were involved actively in the teaching of English in colleges and universities. It was therefore easy to conclude that these poets and novelists were able to use their resources of Western literature, especially English and American, in their own individual creations. A kind of questioning the meaning of life, a sort of interlinking abstraction with concreteness, came through in their poems. On the west coast of India, writing in Marathi, Vinda Karandikar wrote in "The Foundation":

> Athens charged Socrates, well over seventy,
> with corrupting the youth,
> and dragged him before the jury;
> he was pronounced 'guilty' by the majority,
> sentenced to drink poison.

Out of the jury of five hundred and one,
two hundred and twenty
declared him 'not guilty,'
(Sometimes I feel like meeting them,
but this is a digression.)
My optimism
doesn't stand on the two legs of Plato,
but on two hundred twenty into two,
i.e., four hundred and forty legs.

And Gopalkrishna Adiga, who also did his M.A. in English, showed a distinct awareness of the world around him when he said, in "Do Something, Brother":

There's the forest, cut it
clean to the stump, slit it for your buntings.
You have the axe, the sickle, the saw
and the knife; go, harvest all the world
with a flourish of your hand
But
winter mists
light foggy walls that line
the space between your face and mine;
. . . .
No, no, this won't do.
You are a simple man,
and that's your strength.
Horse sense and the blinkers
are your forte.
Eat what comes to the hand;
crush what you touch;
cut the hindering vines.
Mother Earth herself, though tired
lies open to the skies; there's still flesh
upon her bone, marrow for your hunger.
Come, come, brother, never forget
that you are a man!

(A. K. Ramanujan, tr.)

Adiga wrote in his native Kannada and continued to write sensitively, knowingly, until his recent death. No one can miss the beauty in the hidden terror in the above poem, which I have quoted only in part.

The poet, moreover, was no longer a passive onlooker. Changes were taking place everywhere: the seventies saw the imposition of a state of emergency by the then prime minister, Indira Gandhi; terrorism and needless acts of violence became the order of the day in states like Punjab and Assam. Writers and poets had to become one with the anguish they saw and felt. From a quiet lyricism, imagistic patterns in poems changed, and in their place was seen a bolder, freer flow of word and line. I should like to quote in full a poem by the Hindi poet Kunwar Narayan titled "Preparations of War":

> After thousands of years
> like the same beaten-up question
> the same beaten-up man is still being asked
> 'Who are you?
> Where do you live?
> What's your name?'
>
> The prisoner who patrols
> a motionless octagonal cell
> holds three guards captive at the same time.
>
> Everywhere outside
> a forest of iron bars has spread its stranglehold
> like a magnet's invisible lines of force.
>
> And this is the solid proof of the success
> of a massive build-up of arms
> that as soon as we have a gun in our hands
> enemy heads
> begin to appear all around us.
>
> (Vinay and Aparna Dharwadker, trs.)

In Andhra Pradesh, in southeastern India, a poetry calling itself *digambara* or "naked" appeared. This movement in Telugu was uncompromising and scathing and represented a breakthrough in form and content. Interestingly, the first volume of *digambara* verse was released by an unknown rickshaw puller at midnight on a Hyderabad pavement. At the same time, Dalit poetry began to emerge in Maharashtra. The agony in Bapurao Jagtap's lines is unmistakable.

This country is broken into a thousand pieces
its cities, its religion, its castes
its people...
all are broken, fragmented.
...
Let us go to some country, brother,
where, while you live, you will have
a roof above your head,
and where, when you die, there will at least be
a cemetery to receive you.

(Vilas Sarang, tr.)

III

Today, although each region of India has its own language to work with, English continues to be the second most significant medium for literate Indians everywhere. The linking role of English appears almost impossible to do away with, in spite of the ardent protagonists of Hindi; the position of English is certainly vital to the needs of the community, and no one can ignore its growing importance side by side with regional literature.

I said earlier that much poetry has appeared in English over the last thirty years. I find it hard to discover the reasons for this spurt in Indian English writing, but it is a fact that almost half of the total number of books published in India each year are in English. Many or most are not worth mentioning. A disorderly growth, the practitioners of this English verse come from different regions in the country, regions which have their own rich native literatures. There seems to be no link among them and their writings, except for the fact that they all write in English. Once again, as in the case of regional-language poets, the writers of this verse are English academics connected with teaching in universities. Of course there are exceptions, and these are few. But there is no single movement or stance that these Indian English poets pursue; the writing *belongs* to the poet alone, not generally being fuelled by the tensions of the native culture from which the poet comes. Perhaps this has been the primary drawback of much of Indian English poetry until the seventies. But unlike our regional writings, which seem confined to their respective linguistic regions, this literature goes around the country and is read by a sizable number of people. To a certain extent, therefore, English writing can be considered as a national literature, because Hindi is still severely restricted to the northern and central regions of India.

The open, public introspection of a poet's life and family became more or less fashionable in Indian English poetry in the late sixties. Nissim Ezekiel, who is still considered by many as the foremost Indian poet writing in English, had this to say about himself in "Background, Casually": "I went to Roman Catholic school, / A mugging Jew among the wolves. / They told me I had killed the Christ, / That year I won the scripture prize, / A Muslim sportsman boxed my ears." Kamala Das discussed her life and her hungers frankly, almost cruelly, in the manner of poets like Sylvia Plath: "Gift him all, / gift him what makes you woman, / the scent of long hair, / the musk of sweat between the breasts, / the warm shock of menstrual blood / and all your endless female hungers."

For whom did the Indian English poet write? Yes, primarily for Indian readers; but one cannot overrule the fact that the poet also had a Western audience in mind. So, a kind of Indianness was seen in Indian English poems, an Indianness which arises from emotions, habits, and attitudes, giving a certain direction to this poetry. It would be unfair too to slight the desire for such Indianness in English poetry in India, especially when one realises that a conscious striving for Indianness could become a poor substitute for good poetry. As an example, here is a passage from a poem by P. Lal: "Penelope had webs to weave at dead of night, / Sita had fire to see her through— / And you, my love, / What will you do?" A. K. Ramanujan's poetry was pervaded with a sense of Indianness, but it entered quite unconsciously, and with a remarkable sensitivity. Right until his death last year, Ramanujan exhibited a concern for poetic craftsmanship that makes him one of our most satisfying poets writing in English.

However, it was in the midseventies that a change came about in the English poetry written in India. The discerning reader did not wish to read merely a well-crafted poem from an Indian poet, a poem which could have come from a poet in Britain or the USA. Neither was he interested still in the dry wit and irony that most Indian English poems exhibited. The prevailing poetry scene was ready for revaluation. Indian English poets who had been represented in important anthologies (and in special issues of international periodicals) were dropped; in 1976 Oxford University Press published a significant anthology titled *Ten Twentieth Century Indian Poets.* In other words, the era of reassessment had begun. Younger poets from various parts of India were coming out with their poems: suddenly there was Meena Alexander writing from her ancestral background in Kerala, Robin S. Ngangom composing a rooted poetry from the Northeast. It was the native culture that was showing in the poem of the Indian English poet.

IV

I should like to conclude this letter by talking a little about myself, as one living in Orissa, a region with its own rich heritage and culture. It seems natural I would express myself as an Orissan, even though I write in English. My writing would go on to portray cultural values native to Orissa, not to other regions of India. And perhaps I have done just this in my poetry.

But the effort has been difficult. In a region like Orissa, where superstition and irrationality still rule the mind, where the past is the continuing present, where silent masses still have faith in the limbless deity called Jagannath (literally, Lord of the Universe), and where in this area of the Oriya mind, space and time, sound and silence, motion linear and cyclic, and word and symbol become one, the resulting poetry is sure to lose its concreteness, taking the reader to a realm where clarity gets lost, the verse dependent on suggestions of meaning. Maybe this vagueness can put the Western reader off. I have found that poems are often rejected by journals in the West with comments that the poems tend toward the philosophic.

Much of the poetry in English which appeared earlier was marked by a thinness of feeling, without a sense of the tragic that is present in all fine poetry. It is as if the poet were writing from a distance, making the poem a kind of plain verbal exercise. Today, in the early nineties, things are changing. Poets are beginning to take risks with their poems, at the same time sharing their identities with the writers of the region. Caste, hunger, violence, and a fanatical puritanism are aspects of our lives that continue to shame us, even today. It is time that much of our poetry and fiction cease to be inhibited by an inexplicable romanticism.

I would never be wrong if I said that my own poetry has been about Orissa, this land where I was born and have spent all my life. India is too vast a country for one region to know about another. Living beside a slum in the heart of this old, mosquito-infested "city", how could I not have talked about the despair in the eyes of women and children I see every day? How could I not have shared my identity with my neighbour, even though I was educated and wrote in English?

Many of my poems come from true incidents. A poem like "Hunger", which I wrote years ago, could easily happen now as I walk the poverty-ridden sands of the Orissa coastline. The landscape chooses me, and my poems. I may not have written well-crafted poetry at times, but they are words of anguish, my own. And I would like to ask myself: what exactly is the relevance of such poetry to a society which has as its basic problem hunger? I have no answers. With a sense of fatalism one has inherited from one's ancestors, one goes on, aware of how it has moulded one's sensibility. For at the core of all good poetry is the enlargement of our awareness of life, when good poetry acts as a *mantra*, irrespective of whether one looks at it through Western or Indian eyes.

5

Summerdusts and a Scent of Mangoes

When the sun has set, Yajnavalkya, and the moon has set and the fire has gone out and speech has stopped, what serves as a light for a man?

The self, indeed, is his light, for with the self as light he sits, goes out, works and returns.

— from the *Brihadaranyaka Upanishad,* IV.iii.6

Coming back home to India after a six-week-long visit to Japan, I am suddenly struck by the time lag of this tethered country of mine. A sort of dead zone opens in front of me; gone is the synchronous hum of office-goers I experienced the week before in the Tokyo subways, the innocuous oscillations of the weekend crowds at Shinjuku, the purifying grace of cemeteries along the low hill slopes. The nostalgia for the Indian countryside, for the densely tangled green woodland and the blistered ranges of hills stretching away from the water-logged paddies along the coast, now somehow ceases to excite the imagination; a warm moist wind of centuries founders in the weary eyes of the people of this tropical land.

Yes, weary but alive when you watch the five-year-old half-naked child sifting a few grains of rice spilt in the exit drain of the railway restaurant, grinning into the fetid darkness before your eyes. The fuzzy meaningless twilight envelops you as you watch the leper-woman stretch out her mangled palm toward you for a coin, her inner laughter flying in the erratic breeze. Strange that no one feels restless or lost, seeing such things. I should like to believe that an innocence rules us, a reckless innocence, very real and deep, difficult for the occasional visitor to understand. Yet it will not be an untruth to say that many who come from the West do understand and share this seductive power, which enables the people to survive with friendliness and heroism.

It is the beginning of summer here in Orissa, the coastal region on the east where I have spent almost all my life except for short and infrequent visits outside. Mainly agricultural for as long as one can remember, Orissa is now being gradually taken through the process of industrialisation. Orissa, on the Bay of Bengal, with lush jungles and grizzled mountains, at times mellow, at times fearful—endowing it with primitive power. Villages large and small scattered along the many rivers crisscrossing this polytheistic land; rivers which run madly in spate when the savage clouds of the yearly southwest monsoon ruffle up the land, after the long dry summer months, and flood waters engulf the ochre earth in misery. But strangely, the people spring back to their normal existence soon after the calamities; and life goes on the same way as before. One is tempted to ask: is this courage merely a momentary valour that makes them forget their continual hardship, or is it an unfeelingness, a torpor that comes from an acceptance of the law of *karma*—bringing forth a quiet endurance in them, deep and hard and unflinching as the rock which scars this ancient land?

But it is difficult to get any answers. Answers are of no consequence to people here, in a land where the same world goes on and on endlessly, where the rain and the sun seem to do nothing new to the earth, where rituals of old provide the flux of life. But I ask myself questions because I have little faith in me, unlike the millions who believe in their hundreds of gods: a goddess to pray for the boon of a son, a god to beg for a handsome husband, a goddess for riches and so on. These people, among whom I live, they are so unconcerned. And they can suffer one day after another, for a whole lifetime, while the sun and the rain and the earth build their tales, and they rehearse their stories to themselves, discovering those truths that they wish to know.

Now summer is here for four long months, from March through June. It is a hot, humid season when temperatures average 42 degrees Celsius in the shade. The din and bustle of the mornings slowly die down to a drowsy leisure in the afternoons. And mostly the nights are hot and sweaty, too uncomfortable for people to sleep in their small, stuffy houses. And so perhaps the inhabitants of Orissa spend the dark hours in the market-squares, stubbornly watching folk plays based on ancient epics like the *Ramayana* or the *Mahabharata.* By the time the late evening shows at the few cinema halls are giving over, the embellishments and the electric lighting are affixed to the makeshift wooden stages erected at the crossroads of towns and villages. The hot summer night is a challenge, the air impatient for laughter and amusement. Soon the approaches are jammed with men, women and children. All regular traffic shuffles to a halt. Loudspeakers blare. A haunting strain from a *shehnai* heralds a poignant moment from the *Ramayana,* the scene in which Prince Rama is banished from his own kingdom for fourteen long years at the insistence of his cruel stepmother. The packed crowd holds its breath, the women looking to someone other than themselves, nobler than themselves, to redeem them as they view Sita, Rama's wife, meekly following her husband and holding aloft her pure face that suggests a luminous dawn. Particles of time float in the air, separate, then come together. Perhaps this is what breaks the silence of every human being on this festive night: time swelling within the womb of night, silhouetting the unknown territory of the past against the present. So act follows act, as actors turn into gods for a night, eager to bestow faith on those spectators who seem always to need it. And when the eastern horizon shows the wings of light from the rising of the sun, both players and audience leave, to rest and catch up on the sleep they have lost.

Almost anyone from abroad who visits Orissa goes through a whole series of emotions—from sheer shock and disbelief to amazement, and finally to something that seems to enter the being silently, and gives the heart a resignation against the better judgements of the mind—making the visitor aware of this will of the people to *live.* A time-inherited people, living amidst temples and shrines, with their fairs and festivals, feasts and fasting; and growing through disastrous cyclones and famines into the deep-rooted tradition of their ancestors. Look into the faces trudging along the dusty, pitted roads—perhaps faces of bodies that have been going without proper food for two days—you will notice that their eyes are quick and warm and alive, like oil lamps burning, throwing around them their tiny worlds of beaten gold! There, in the burning heat of noon, the farmer stands, frail and naked, looking down at the little patch of his land; but it is the light in his eyes that you notice, burning pure as water; from her numb village hut the new bride takes slow close steps to the river, her warm alert breath filling the empty pitcher cradled in her arm; and the men speak a language of summerdusts, its light scattered by the scents of mangoes, like an aura of hyacinths rising from numerous village pools. In dark quiet evenings they remember the dead men who never leave them lonely; the fires of evening with their illusion of light.

For essentially India is a land obsessed with light. Particularly Orissa, with its bias for sun-worship that has bound the people for hundreds of years. Far away from the recognised tourist centres of the country, perhaps the inaccessible, comfortless countryside of Orissa deters the visitor. Along the coast, the sea is a meditating blue as a brilliant sun urges it from nowwhere to break its surface in myriad glints of silver. The wind is a dogged, cool caress even in the heat of day. The coastline is flat and the bold light leaps from one fiery crown to another of the rows of coconut palms greening the land as far as the eye can see. Pariah kites slowly circle above as stray white summer clouds drift on high in the skies, away from the pulsating urgency of hunger on the ground, and in the fishermen's shoddy shacks along the sandy beaches, where naked bodies are prisoners of themselves. Deeper inland the banyans take root like giants, extending their mysterious limbs into the air, standing guard like sentinels from some bygone era; while on the earth the stubborn grass frets and sways and the mimosas droop into sleep at the touch of unknown presences. And on a deserted stretch of sand stands the monumental temple to the Sun God, shaped as a gigantic chariot. The twenty-four magnificently carved stone wheels, the seven proud horses pulling this massive edifice; are those symbols of time our ancestors forged in fear and love to overcome their world? What does it promise? A journey into the unknown, an end, or an uncontrolled amazement? All I know is that I live in a timeless country as I wait for whatever it is that would tell me where I have come from and what I am going to be. And that is the pattern of life that stays in my memory.

Yet polytheistic though India is, all religious belief in Orissa strangely points to one god—to the temple of Jagannath at Puri, the scene of the famed chariot festival, when the grotesque limbless deity of Jagannath is ceremoniously taken out every year for his symbolic tour of the universe, to study the fate of mankind. To my mind, Jagannath remains the most primitive of gods, having his origins in the rituals of savage tribes of the dense Orissa forests. For here were the ambiguous essences symbolised and made into ritual objects. The totem soon became the escape of the dark will into freedom. The shape was necessary for worship, for contemplation; a shape as primitive today as it was three thousand years ago: a stark log of wood with huge circles for eyes, minus hands or feet; a shape that moves you as you stare at it, moving darkly and circling, and drawing you with the ropes of your breath into a country of your own making where you stand, transfixed, saying to yourself: "Do what you want, I am ready. Join my life."

But I was speaking of summer. This year it hasn't been as warm as in previous years. Almost every week, around late afternoon, a wild wind blows in suddenly from the west, along with threatening swells of dark rain clouds. The sun dies out, thunder rumbles ominously overhead, savage gusts of wind throw objects here and there. Inside the house, I run to shut the doors and windows. Dust seems to be everywhere; it enters the nostrils and stings the eyes. Cyclists on the roads are thrown off balance; ageing trees lie uprooted disrupting traffic. And then the rain of a summer storm seems to pour all over the earth, lashing everything in its path. The air smells of ozone, of fish and seaweed. Then the rain stops as suddenly as it had begun. It has become cool, the temperature dropping to the twenties. Outside are little pools on the ground to cool the bare feet of children dashing after the joy of uprooted things. I look out the window and see two crows, wet and shivering, on a tall branch of the deodar in the yard. A magpie robin calls sweetly from a nearby bush. The mango tree looks darker with raindrops on the leaves; the green fruit hang lower with the extra weight of water on them. The wet earth touches me, leaves of my heart dripping. Above me, the sky trembles with a new measure of space. I glimpse something there, like my mind, afloat—the truth of old legends and epics, slipping between reality and dream.

Cuttack, where I was born and grew up by the bank of a river beside that dark-bellied temple, which stands today, dark and drowsy, as though asleep. Cuttack, the dusty, malarial town lying in a bowl of humble valley between two rivers—where I grew up, spent my boyhood and youth. Cuttack, that brings me face to face with my memories. Cuttack, where the tired footprints of my long dead grandfather still remind me of his hunger and anguish. Once, years ago, his footprints would have left their agitated trail in the unmade paths of this land. As he ran on, suffering uncontrollably from hunger, away from the frayed fabric that the famine had made of his life—he was picked up, shrunk to bone, by some white missionaries, and entered a time of new religion and unease. Cuttack, my poem of long memory, where tuberculosis stilled the pearly body of the thirteen-year-old girl before her breasts had bloomed to purity. Where hundreds of lepers still shuffle along the dirty roads, begging from door to door, and believing in their heart of hearts that they *are* suffering for the sins they had committed in their previous lives. Where the slender but starving whore brazenly searches for customers on hot summer nights. Cuttack, with its ruined, battle-scarred fort, surrounded by a moat now clogged with weeds and slime. And where the old banyan tree still stands by the river, its trunk frayed, its branches gasping for air—the tree from whose high boughs criminals were hanged in the old days. . .

Who would seriously consider now writing ornamental, romantic stuff akin to the ancient Sanskrit? Yet, perhaps, some continue to write in that vein, urged on by the aural poetry of the epics, that lives on via the performing arts. I remember the following lines by an Orissan poet in praise of poetry:

> Poetry is a sensitive woman
> whose father is the poet
> But whose midwife lays her bare.

The true measure of her worth
        is recognized
Only when she is enjoyed
        by an exalted man of learning.
An idiot is merely
        a malicious stepbrother to her.

Without relevance to our society today, this poetry only empties itself. Hunger and sexuality remain our basic issues. It remains to *us* to talk of such things.

For nothing is clean here but grief.

With the sense of destiny one encounters at every step, one appears to hold one's birth in one's hand. It is the dead in India who debase the living; and the people continue to think that they have the right to do so—an example of an innocence which carries them motionless forever through vague tomorrows.

Out there in the street, under a warm sticky sun, a tourist from a far-off land walks about aimless, seeking repose in the white haze of unyielding stone; the seventeenth beggar-woman of the morning is becoming another face on an empty coastline that will continue to haunt him (unlike the rich bronze he is going to carry back as a priceless souvenir for his living room) as a momentary stab of conscience. And conscience, too, is the feel of the melted tar of the street against the soles of his Florsheims, the smell of cigarettes and beer, the perfect lines of kohl on Lakshmi's taunting eyelids, and babies' cries sprinkled in the sun. And as the tourist walks to his car idling in the street, he thinks it's too much bother, trying to be *us* as well as himself—perhaps holding his breath in mild wonder as he sees through the ritual farce we play to the ghosts of our ancestors we will surely become.

His car meanders through the chaotic traffic and suddenly comes to a halt at the common enough sight of a bull chasing a cow. Ahead, the street is almost clear, pedestrians having given way for the two creatures to copulate. Time's stubborn voice persists. In the people's eyes, this is still in part a sacred sight. A group of young schoolgirls in navy blue pinafores give shy glances as they whisper self-consciously to one another. It is a scene the visitor finds hard to take in. But this is the rural India

I live in, another of the endless *mantras* of survival. I remember a passage from the *Brihadaranyaka Upanishad:*

> In the embrace of his beloved a man
> forgets the whole world,
> everything within and without;
> in the very same way, he who embraces the Self
> knows neither within nor without.

To what end, one wonders. Toward what grace which eludes me as much as it does the self-seeking tourist? One is awed when one observes the sinuous men and women, gods and goddesses, clinging erotically to one another on temple walls; exquisite and sensuous figures in granite, they end there. For when one enters the inner sanctum, the walls are bare except for the deity in the centre. Strange how a sense of a perfect whole is experienced through a synthesis of opposites: through thought and action, cause and effect, through the man-woman principle of *ardhanarishwar:* half man, half woman.

Now as I come to the end of this, I realise that I have merely been walking back and forth along these paths, losing myself like light in river and sky, asking for pain like my fellow beings. Perhaps it is a poem I crave for, an illusive alphabet that betrays with words upon a page. The air above the street beyond starts to tremble in the day's heat, and the sun is going up over the rooftops and coconut palms. And the crows are flying in and out, picking up scraps of food, flying into more crows. Another morning, I tell myself, waking to dream.

The day passes by. Perhaps I am too awake. Or perhaps all that I have written exists only in my mind. Or am I merely playing in the light, reaching for stars, feeling layer on layer on layer of time? It is difficult to take refuge in a faith my people understand. It becomes difficult to replace myself. I don't know what to believe in: but maybe in what we face in one another, what we do to one another—and even that gives off an air of sadness. . . like the scent of mangoes in the sluggish morning breeze. Maybe a faith comes into being in the self, moment by moment, within a stone, a leaf, a face, an empire or a legend, within an instant that extends itself over the hour; within anything that makes you forget its power, sweeping you on to your destiny.

6

The Inaudible Resonance of English Poetry in India

"Everything implies a universe."

— Borges

I

Uncertain as I am in my very existence, I feel uncomfortable in making any sort of statement about poetry in general, and about my own work. For as a practising writer (if I can call myself that), even after years of continual struggle I see myself suddenly faced with the inconsistent character of my poetry. This, my realisation of my incompetence, becomes a strong ground for dissatisfaction, a sore that often festers to dismiss the workings of my imagination as irrelevant. Such times throw one into a state of despair. And what other course is left open then but to treat myself to a period of total humility?

It is this treatment (I wonder whether it is a sort of posturing) that helps me to bounce back to work again with renewed determination, while in reality I am aware that there has been no change, simply a renewed flight of birds.

A basic uncertainty makes it difficult to bring forth an impersonal assessment of one's own art, however and in whatever ways an artist may choose to try. Such determination of absolutes (which may be called 'truths') only holds good for scientific matters, and does not appear tenable for literature, because the same criteria cannot be applied for both. The primary reason for this appears to lie in the emotive content of all literature. It might arise from the fact that various experiences at various times in the writer's life have clothed the essentiality of his being, which the writer exploits in symbols of his own making, thereby placing him in a situation which fails to isolate him sufficiently in order that he see himself as he really is. The process of writing has moulded him to react to emotion in a different way; and perhaps, he too, like his work, releases emotion in a different way. Hence it would not be wrong to state that a writer is incapable of a clear and objective vision of his work; and if one extrapolates this statement further, to say that he is even incapable of making himself properly understood. And yet, writers everywhere have started at almost the same emotional stage—for has the reaction of any writer to the sight of his own first book been different from any other's? The type may be blunt, the paper may be shoddy, and the magazine may be a six-page duplicating-machine job, but there *it* is, growing perceptibly in dimension before him, to be admired by him and perhaps his closest friends—simply because it contains his first work in print. Can any writer be objective then? Gradually, however, as the writer proceeds from work to work, from book to book, he is caught up in a web from which he cannot escape; and although his initial excitement has subsided, he begins to be drawn into an inner world of his own making—a world spaced by his own life, of secret allusions, of desire and agony, of a constantly changing alignment between dream and reality which makes it nearly impossible for him to demand an understanding into his future. In essence, the artist fails to assess the dominion of his art, because his art itself has readied him with the sort of defence-mechanism which ultimately clips his wings.

Nevertheless, it is this process of development of his own art which pushes the serious writer along, and of which he is acutely, agonisingly conscious: to find that aspect of his work which will ennoble and promise. He might not be able to come close to his ideal, he might not be able to produce that work which can be labelled as 'great', largely influenced by the enormity of his immediate universe which places his work at a particular point in space-time. This then becomes his weakness: his incapability of walking across the sphere of influence of that point, bogged by his self-avowed objectivity, and finally only being able to place his art into that condition from which he cannot liberate it. Thus, as the writer plods his gruelling track, in the fervent hope that at some point in his life he produce his ideal 'classic', the very realisation of what he has been trying to do (against the 'greats' before him) forces him into a nagging hostility with himself, making him painfully *accept* the greatness of the work in front of him, and ultimately drawing him into the ordeal of his silence that becomes his refuge. And, where he discovers that his own development of the theme he has been working on is not as objective as he wanted it to be; for the 'eternity' he has spent coming there has merely succeeded in revealing an indifferent language, or a watered-down copy of that exemplary work of art he held so dear . . .

I feel the same way about my writing too; my so-called objective language, only, pathetically reveals my very indifference. How has such an indifference crept into my writing without my being aware of it? Has it come from an improper use of the language itself, or from the tradition I am used to in my own life and literature? Or have these two factors conspired together to reveal the deficiency of the human spirit in my poetry? It is truly hard to replace personal history by history-at-large. Perhaps I am unable to judge my own humanity; or, if I am able to see it, it is only up to a point. But to celebrate it, through feeling and language which pass on the mythic forces of life so that the completed work transcends time and place, places much greater demands upon the imagination which are never likely to be met.

My origins lie in the lower middle class, my upbringing was in a narrow, rural community; and I learnt my English in a missionary school from a British schoolmaster. I studied Mathematics and Physics, and later trained to be a physicist; I was far away from the academic world of English literature. Now, when I look back at the years behind me, the thought that I would write poetry in English at one time seems unbelievable. I started writing poetry rather late in life, at an age when most poets would have normally shelved their creation in a drawer, and basked in the mellow shapings of their art. But there was this sudden urge in me, to write; and today as I pursue my restless course of drifting across misty seas of thought, I realise I cannot trust my talent to bring me to shore: to close in on the ideal of a classic that every serious writer aspires to accomplish in his lifetime. But perhaps I *am* approaching closer; and as I grope from poem to poem for the key to human understanding, at times it becomes painfully obvious that the bits and pieces of the nature of existence which I give place to in a poem, have become incapable of integration, incapable of coalescing into a haunting whole. For until such a process is achieved in any work, until this fragmented, crafted experience of the writer portrays a unified vision, thereby acquiring the right to challenge the commonplace acts and properties of life, and compels him to use time as lavishly (and wastefully) as he can, the classic which he strives to create will not come about.

Now, how does a writer in his unending pursuit of creation turn 'critical?' In other words, when does the writer feel that he is on the point of producing his masterpiece? Or, does he feel anything at all? And afterwards?

These are questions once again the reactions to which will vary from person to person, from artist to artist; any generalised judgement cannot, possibly, be made. We are human beings who have been born from, and to, a fundamental uncertainty; proceeding within an uncertainty. A cry, a flash of joy, a sudden crisis like death or a betrayal—situations as these set certain limits on our sense and appetite, which, consciously or not, teach us to discriminate differently, to weigh the world in our own, privately-oriented ways. Hence it becomes impossible to predict how and when a writer reaches that 'critical' condition when he may create his great work of art.

Yet, we are, much too much, carried away by the opinions of others, by the talk of critics, who, once again, have been shaped by their own singular limitations. On the other side, the statement that it takes an artist to understand an artist is a wild one. One need not agree with Ezra Pound that the only valid critic is the creative artist, to recognise how significant are the verdicts of a gifted critic who is both a critic and a writer. Still, art remains essentially a matter of the imagination, and critics somehow have always seemed to veer away from the imaginative vein of a writer's work. To a large extent, it is the critics who have to share part of the responsibility—of not being able to contribute towards the making of a classic. (Here I am referring to Indian critics in particular—both in English and in the regional Indian languages.) Ranking a poet is often intolerable to many a lesser poet, making him adopt other means for elevating himself in the public eye; often it is rhetoric, or gesture, less often abstraction. Each one of us uses words on his own intellectual level, and the resolute drive to produce a 'great' or 'classic' piece of work might help him to raise that level. If the writer succeeds, the attempt to do so puts him to considerable strain. The writer begins to lose a crucial part of himself. I have, in the recent past, been harrowingly pitted against this urgency of working on a significant poem, quite different from my other books, and I have felt the steady, salient erosion in me, the torment of struggle unbearable at times. The pressures are so urgent that one would gladly throw away one's life and art to attain that illusory ideal of a classic piece of art. I shall discuss this poem of mine later. But now, finally that the poem is over and done, and I come to see myself and my own work in the related literary mosaic of the time, the realisation itself has become a much desired, but agonising lesson.

II

It would be interesting to observe now as to how close English poetry in India has come to this ideal of classic poetry. The thinness of our poetry has come to be an established fact. It cannot be denied that nothing spectacular has emerged from years of our written poetry—nothing that in any manner resembles the nature of a classic. True, the voice is there, inside, and it comes to the poet, feeling its way, but once it appears on the printed page, it fails to establish a relationship with the reader. Perhaps the voice is a safe one, strongly bound to its ties and mannerisms, handed over to the Indians by the revered British poets. Neatly done, the poems lack the creative indirectness of approach that is the measure of true poetry. Where is the building up of an experience and its pursuit to the very end, as has been done so successfully in some of the Indian languages? Where *is* the singular intuition into the human condition in our poetry? Where is that clairvoyance that works intensely, kaleidoscopically—to celebrate the awe and mystery of the human condition?

We have to admit that such an intuition is decidedly absent in Indian poetry written in English, today. Reasons are hard to find for this state which seems both emotionally and intellectually empty. For where is the pure idea in our poetry? All poems flooding the magazines are characterised by sameness and thinness; one poem reads as weakly as another: poems limited to pale, colourless accounts arising out of commonplace encounters in everyday lives. Such poems come about as a result of a sudden response to things—poems capable of a limited sphere of influence—slight and jaundiced, which do not conspire from a harmonious horizon of living and being. And one seldom sees a poem where a single experience is explored from beginning to end in Indian poetry in English.

Is it therefore from a genuine lack of crises in the Indian milieu that the 'great' experience is not pursued through the medium of English? Or, is it that the fault lies in the poet's use of the language itself? Or, is the majority of our poets merely interested in a sort of self-entertainment for their own selves and for their few friends, and have no wish to be read and appreciated beyond their own immediate circles?

For, crisis, as the word is commonly understood, has possibly less relevance for the Indian than for his Western counterpart. There is no doubt that the Indian mind is passive and compliant; and the Indian tends to overcome any crisis with a falsely superior reliance on the power of destiny. (I may be wrong, conscious that my statement leaves much room for error.) And it might be that a want of real crises in the writer's life weakens the force of his commitment to himself, preventing him from getting close to the 'ideas' that matters in the writing of poetry. These 'ideas' are rooted in the poet's convictions about the world in which he exists, and offer an effective presence of himself in the objects around him. This presence must have the power to release the poet, a release which passes effectively into the poet's 'vision'. The poet's vision may come to the poet 'miraculously' as a revelation; or may come about slowly, revealing to the poet the order of his own making, as he plods from poem to poem; a kind of assurance of the self that is achieved finally not merely by imagination and by language. It *is* a purity of the self, this vision of the poet; by virtue of which his consciousness grows clearer, things and feelings all fall into place. One remembers keenly the late Hugh MacDiarmid's words to achieve desperately this 'unity' in poetry:

The function, as it seems to me,
Of poetry is to bring to be
At long, long last that unity.

Every serious poet tries to do something of this sort in every single poem he makes. But what he actually accomplishes is another matter. The greatest poetical works of our time have been nourished by such ideas: ideas epitomising the work of Dante and Whitman, of Neruda and Seferis. While it is true that at that time too, other writers were also consistently producing good work, their poetry lacks significance and doesn't reach greatness because of an absence of such 'ideas' in them, because the ideas in their work were weak and commonplace. This labels their poetry as 'minor'.

Still, to call poets 'major' or 'minor' seems unwise, and acts as an awful ridicule to any poet. It does play a sort of havoc on an aspiring poet, inducing various reactions in him. A really great poet will never be affected by such utterances, though. And yet, the ability to take criticism creates the ground for the build-up of a true artist. Many writers, I am sure, will not agree with my statement—because being a great artist does not necessarily imply that he be callous and indifferent to criticism, but that he should realise when it's time to dismiss a critic's stance as irrational and playful. For, in essence, the greatness of an artist has far back been decided upon by the genes which run the anxious blood through his veins, a matter already shaped by biochemical factors in the amniotic landscape of his mother's womb. The lack of a live critical tradition is a disturbing feature of English poetry in our country, and is greatly responsible for the mediocrity and general confusion that prevails. Except for stray, sporadic poems dating to the nineteenth century, contemporary English poetry had nothing sacred to fall back upon. Hence the sentiments existing in Georgian verse served as grandiose examples for many of our Indian poets. Based mainly in the important Indian cities, these writers generally reflected the plight of the Westernised Indian. Not being exposed to the traditional literatures of India in the regional languages, the English poet has no awareness of the human history, of the tissues of sensibility and thought, of belief and experience, which exists in the living literatures of our languages. The poet is undoubtedly alienated; he is incapable of fishing from the classical literatures primarily because he has no knowledge of any regional language other than English. He is oblivious of myth, and perhaps of the epic tradition of the rural Indian. The Indian past is, therefore, a dead past for the Indian poet writing in English, and becomes a pathetic simplification of his state of existence. It seems natural to conclude that a poet with a live cultural past behind him, aware of his roots and perhaps prejudiced by those roots, has a greater probability of writing significantly than one who has no knowledge of any Indian language other than English. In other words, a bilingual writer, can, with persistent effort, produce poetry of a fundamental reality which embraces the human condition—but only if he is at home with the English language and feels that he is not writing for a foreign English-speaking audience. The latter is an important point which cannot be overemphasized. Most English poetry in this country fails because our poets are simply unaware of the society from which the poetry emerges; because being city poets they deal with the basically uninspiring middle-class, and their poetry turns out to be equally uninspiring; they produce a kind of 'willed' poetry that is forced out of their selves and which ignores the rural psyche. For only when this human condition is embodied in the right language, the poetry tends toward the epic or classic nature.

I would like to conclude this essay by stating that Indian poetry has, until now, not reached any measure of success in approximating to the ideal of classic or great poetry. The poetry remains, fundamentally, a thick undergrowth, but unable to satisfy the demands of the earth which bears it. It is easy to cite examples of good, competent poems in the poetry of Daruwalla, or Ezekiel, or Parthasarathy, or Ramanujan—but they are never near the definition of a classic. The competent practitioners only show how weak, and how occasional, our poetry is today. There is very little passion in the poetry of Ezekiel; and many of the younger poets write after him. A poetry that is safe and institutionalised can never expand, can never reach the 'classic' boundaries. Nobody can deny that our poets fail miserably to go into the Indian psyche, and to feel what brings about the contradictions in the Indian character. On the other side, we see younger poets who are not interested in language at all, but employ gesture—which implies a principle of poetry that exists outside of its embodiment in words. We also observe an undue use of irony and satire (does this follow too from the British poets?)—the sly leer in the poem, which goes contrary to the Indian character and makes it simply effective caricature. Which is that poem in English where the emotion and thought generated in its lines goes beyond the boundaries of the poem? Which is that poem that possesses a significance beyond the ordinary, and which makes of one's own predicament a universal one?

Two poems or books, published recently, come to my mind because their approach is radically different from others, and because they soften as the poems respond to our reading. Both books are, in a sense, pilgrimages. They are Arun Kolatkar's *Jejuri* and R. Parthasarathy's *Rough Passage.* They can be thought of as coming near to our idea of 'classics'. And yet, both are embedded in their small, limited feelings. Perhaps, *Rough Passage* would be worthwhile to examine here, as, by the poet's own admission, it took twenty years to complete. It is the poet's only book. And because of twenty years continued effort given to the poem, it might approach our ideal. The poem is a long one, and is woven around an 'idea'—an idea about the 'burdens' of the poet's roots. But a close examination reveals that this idea never develops beyond an early promise, in spite of skilled, peacock-plumed imagery, perhaps because of an element of sentimentality that echoes through the different sections of the poem—or simply because the poet fails to *illuminate* his experience and just goes on mirroring it; and thus ultimately fails to set forth the meaningful aspects of experience from the transient one. On the other hand, if one compares *Rough Passage* with Dante's *Divine Comedy,* for instance; Dante's work appears to move much much beyond his historical moment. The power of Dante's description is enormous, supported by his intense learning that synthesizes his imagination into the quality of an epic. Parthasarathy talks of his Tamil culture in a poetry of self-consciousness that ultimately binds him and his craft; restricting the movement of the poem, and thereby becomes incapable of transcending that self-consciousness. The reader looks at Parthasarathy's 'idea' but does not succumb to it; the reader is not coaxed into any manner of sustained retrospection: for does the end of *Rough Passage* tempt us to go back, into the poem again? If, as the poet insists, *Rough Passage* is to be read as a single, unified book, its conclusion must sustain the experience contained in the work. We cannot be certain of this. 'Homecoming', the final section of the book, in short, serves to leave us nowhere as it were, without urging us back to the book's beginning, and preventing any exchange with 'Exile', the first section of the poem.

This was never intended to be a criticism of *Rough Passage,* but a comparison of sorts to show that no poem perhaps has been writen which can be called a classic. And yet this is the only contemporary poem which approaches that ideal. For although *Rough Passage* is a single piece of work, it does not offer its readers a prolonged reading experience, but a variety of feelings. Our poets (and I am very much among them) are still powerless of integrating their experience; so the poetry remains a process—fragmentary, like an unfinished argument. Earlier, I said, that I have tried to write such a poem; a poem which might offer its readers a single, fused reading experience, but its success seems limited when I look back on it. How far one 'accomplishes' things rests more on others, not on the writer. This poem of nearly 500 lines, which I have simply titled *Relationship,* shall be published late next year. I would not like to think more about it now. Too many people care *too much* about their poems, *their* reputations. This preoccupation is a foreseen one in a society such as ours, a static society that appears incapable of growing up—and it eventually chokes the process of writing poems.

I believe that a culture (of which I am a part) has its dreams, and continues to provide the symbolic terms of our existence. My poem, *Relationship,* a product of dreams, has made me speak of the demands of a pilgrimage— threatened by the living Oriya past, by nagging hunger and by a persistent sexuality. I realise I am answerable to my own creation of this reality of my imagination, and to the logicality of my ideas. I also realise that these should help in making readers more aware and conscious of their existence. But imagination is a monstrous computer, it confounds more than it clarifies. Our sense has its limits. Bound as we are, severely by space and time, by the past and future, our imagination and our understanding is always incomplete—making of that 'reality' an uncertain one, something that makes one always a stranger on the scene the writer chooses to depict.

7

Recent Commonwealth Fiction: Writing from Three Different Cultures

Would it be right, I wonder, to say that much of the best writing in English (both in fiction and poetry) is being done outside the British and American traditions? London and New York have, in the last few years, ceased to be the strongholds of writing; have in fact, stopped to dictate the norms of such writing in English. And yet it is true that several recognised writers of the Commonwealth no longer live in their own countries but have chosen to live in England or America; or, do reside for intermittent periods away from their homelands. (This they do for various reasons, which can be discussed separately.) By a Commonwealth writer we refer to a writer from one of the former British colonies—in other words, a writer from *usually* one of the poor and developing countries (ours included)—countries which have absorbed and outlasted the superior Western experience (technologically superior, that is). These writers have something new to offer because of their distinct new consciousness; and it also arises from the fact that their thinking has been somehow sanctified, as though from flames that accompanied the births of their own nations. Today, therefore, it may not be out of place to call their roles significant; this because they seem to hold forth hopes tenable in the context of a world irreparably torn by conflict, scepticism and boredom; more because of *the* quality of tenderness which seems to feed the strength of such works of fiction.

Some examples of recent Commonwealth fiction that have become more meaningful (to me as a reader) than the rush of post-modernistic literatures especially from the United States and Western European countries, are from the African countries, from Australia and the West Indies, and also from New Zealand. They appear more worthwhile because of a conservative moral potency that outdoes in many ways the purposelessness so much manifest in the record of writings of late twentieth-century man. It is quite true that literature everywhere (since 1900) has reflected social change. The anonymity of urban life has produced fiction of alienation and dereliction, and the more permissive morality while introducing new freedoms, has also brought new uncertainties. While in the mechanised West, rural settings for works of fiction have gradually disappeared.

When Baudelaire wrote:

> With a happy heart I climbed the hill from where
> The city can be seen in its fullness...
> I wanted to intoxicate myself with the vast whore
> Whose infernal charm unceasingly makes me young again...
> I love you, O infamous capital! Harlots and gangsters,
> You often hold out pleasures that the profane
> Masses cannot understand.

He emphasised the ugliness, the perversity (more than anyone else perhaps) as he went on to glorify the city. In contrast, these writers from the Commonwealth, whose works of fiction I have chosen, use distinctly rural settings; further, their work is rooted in a signficant reality. I would like to pick up two unknown writers (at least fairly unknown in India)—one from New Zealand and the second from Nigeria—to (1) see how an Indian reader like myself reacts to such literature, and (2) place their fiction beside the work of an Indian writer (in my opinion the most outstanding), i.e., R.K. Narayan. *These writers all base their fiction on a ground of realism.* They have no use for fantasy, or for the modernist techniques of anonymity inspired by the industrial and urban behaviour of Western society.

Witi Ihimaera is the first Maori to have written a novel in English. *Tangi,* which has the distinction of being this novel, also (incidentally) was awarded the first prize in the 1974 James Wattie 'Book of the Year' Award. His collection of short stories, *Pounamu, Pounamu,* and his second novel, *Whanau,* were also warmly received by readers and critics alike.

From a different culture comes Obi B. Egbuna, the young Nigerian playwright and fiction writer. He is different from Ihimaera in that he is a master of the ancient art of story-telling. Of his collections of stories, *Daughters of the Sun* and *Emperor of the Sun* are worthy of note. His latest novel is called *The Minister's Daughter.*

Ihimaera, Egbuna and Narayan—three writers from three totally different cultures—are linked by the fact that they all belong to the Commonwealth. (And what a misnomer the word *commonwealth* is, because the three writers come from backward, poor nations!) Their cultures are ancient; they have a strong oral tradition of story-telling and of song; and this is what makes it crucial—they are all natives of their lands. Their use of English could be rather limited, since they were not born to the language—but this limitation itself makes the use of the English language in their work more subtle and challenging, their having adopted successfully certain techniques of today's English-speaking writers in the West.

Witi Ihimaera's novel, *Tangi,* is a simple account of the death of an old man, the father of the young man, Tama, who is presented as the hero in the novel. The entire book is narrated in the first person, and it is done without formality—very casually as it were—the author's own experience held, and compelled into art. Death is what affirms the exercise of life, and this is what *Tangi* demonstrates, through the age-old Maori values placed on life; and Ihimaera has been able to show this through *aroha,* through love and loneliness and sympathy that people have for one another. Very simply *Tangi* begins:

> This is where it ends and begins. Here, on the railway station, Gisborne, waiting for the train to Wellington. Here begins the first step into the future, the first step from the past. I am alone now. So long reliant on father, so long my hand in his; now myself, my own keeper, for his hand has slipped away.

Tangi might not be called a major novel; yet it is one of the warmest and most honest novels I have read in a long time. The book is vivid in its portrayal of the village family unity of rural Maori life, and as the reader progresses through the book he is engagingly drawn into living itself, into a more moral and meaningful world of the mind that seems so much absent from the recent fiction of our time. Ihimaera, with his readily accessible poetic prose in which narration, dialogue and memories weave passionately into one another, takes the reader right into the centre of Maori life—the lush land, the traditional values of his people—at the same time knowing and letting us know that such values will slowly and certainly be lost. In fact, the prose is charged at times with blind, hot emotional peaks that shoot up as though from a carrier frequency of earthbound sadness that forms the backdrop of the book. The overall effect is almost incantatory:

The lights are on in Waituhi and people run through the mud and rain busying themselves for the tangi. There is so much to do and there is little time to weep. It is best to keep on doing something, anything, to keep the grief away.

> Aue. Aue...
> This is the cry of sadness.
> Aue. Aue...
> This the keening of women on the marae, waiting
> to welcome the visitors to the tangi.
> Aue. Aue...
> And this is the cry of my own heart breaking.
> E pa, he has gone from me. I am alone. For three days,
>
> I will see him lying still on the marae. For three days, I will remember how good he was to me. Then on the third day, he will be buried on the Hill. Aue. Aue...

Such mourning sounds almost Indian; the prose has a chanting, hypnotic quality. (I would say more like the rural life in Orissan or other villages of South India.) Thus, immersed in the reading of the novel, I almost forgot that I was Indian and not Maori. And this is perhaps how a reader coming from a rural culture like ours relates to literature from far-off New Zealand. Would a similar reaction come from a reader, say, from a developed European country or from one adapted to highly urbanised city life?

One, therefore, reaches the end of *Tangi* in the mode of going through a long ritual—a ritual that never ceases to lose its primitive importance for the reader. In such a society the son has begun to take up the role of the dead father. And that is how it should be: 'Slowly, life was beginning again. The call to go on living became more insistent.' *Tangi* has no brilliantly ingenious handling of plot; from beginning to end it remains a story of a rural burial. And the novel's beauty rests on the simple world of family relationships—so much more understood, more satisfying to us because we lead similar lives here in India—and so very real because the account of death becomes, quite simply, an affirmation of life...

Leaving this story of Maori village life (with the feeling that death helps man to live on in this world), we turn to Obi B. Egbuna's fiction. Egbuna is an excellent short story writer; he knows his craft well. One immediately becomes aware of the basically aural traditions of the African, and feels that here is one who is simply continuing the ancient practice of story-telling but only through a different medium. However, Egbuna's themes are modern and set in the Africa of today. He is adept at bringing forth the Africa of legend and springing a surprise on the reader; all the while you are painfully aware that Obi Egbuna is laughing quietly behind your back. In the story 'Divinity' from his earlier collection of stories, *Daughters of the Sun,* an elderly catechist challenges the power of the village 'Divinity' with terrible results. The story concludes thus:

> Catechist Thomas, now peering meekly through a window, wondered why most things in life often began as an answer without a question and usually end up a question without an answer. He sighed helplessly... And then, as if from the archives of the dead, a voice that sounded anything but human, a voice that focused your imagination on immortality whether you liked it or not, the 'tangible' voice of the Ebunu Juju, began a weird solo.

'The Medics', from the same collection, shows another aspect of his art. An American medical student (his white jacket bearing a Harvard University athletic badge) has come to Africa as a Peace Corps volunteer and confronts a traditional tribal leader, who is a 'witch-doctor' to him. The story is done through deft dialogue—between the two—and is amusing yet disquieting at the same time. Obi Egbuna demonstrates at the end of the tale how the so-called witch-doctor's powers are greater than those of his Western counterpart: for he has 'created imagination'—something that the American possibly cannot comprehend. And throughout the entire confrontation Egbuna's touches of satire show as light flicks of a whip at the snobbery of the Peace Corps worker; the end comes as a final, firmer stroke at the idle incredulity of the American.

'Rivers Can't Speak' from Egbuna's new collection, *Emperor of the Sea,* is pure story. Across a backdrop of legendary Africa Egbuna shows how the old still remain superior to the young, to the very ends of their lives. With wry humour the writer establishes this myth in the reader's mind; one is forced to realise that the old *are* the true inheritors of the earth. The river is Egbuna's triumph, appearing real: 'if only they could speak...' And Egbuna (it is he, none else!) who asks, 'I like old men, don't you? They make me think of so much that was good that has gone.'

Egbuna's stories are masterpieces in the craft of story-telling. The powerful narration, so much of it oral, grips the reader in its flow. And yet, Egbuna does not seem to reach the intense peaks of emotion which Ihimaera achieves so easily in his gentle writing. What makes Egbuna's work weaker is the emphasis on irony; and basically on the differences of race and class which appear to eat into the writer's soul—making the final outcome look bleak and inhibited. One is left with a bitter taste on the tongue: of Egbuna's obsessive approach to writing that seems to have come as a result of years of colonisation, of being held 'inferior' to the European or the American. Here truly, Egbuna's art becomes his act of experience, and therefore perhaps fails.

It would be of much interest now to examine these two writers in the light of R.K. Narayan's work. (I have not quoted from Narayan in any detail as most of us are familiar with his work.) Narayan is a natural story-teller who portrays quite another world: of Indian town-life very different from these two. With mature realism every little part of his stories expresses the wholeness of the Indian condition—with its hopes and anxieties—with the dreamlike desire to turn inwards if not also toward the past that still *is* so much a part of our lives. It is because Narayan's fiction reflects honestly the stuff of which our lives are made and ordered. His language is graceful, and he writes from the inside of a small town-life he seems to know so well. He has no use for the irony of Egbuna. Amusing at times, Narayan's tolerant picture of Indian life never attains the sour and derisive flavour that darkens the writings of other Commonwealth writers—as for example, in the work of Jhabvala and Naipaul. This is where Narayan differs from the other novelists, and from Egbuna as well. For Narayan's novels, from *The Bachelor of Arts* to *The Painter of Signs*, are written with the perfect vision of an insider.

Thus Narayan works to a certain order, of quiet tolerance, from within the Indian tradition: an order in which confusion might result from following the voices of reason. There is an inherent realism; and if this realism brings about with it a loss of hope or fulfilment, it also surprises one into living for some other purpose—as Raman's aunt discovers toward the end of *The Painter of Signs*.

Ihimaera, Egbuna and Narayan have all worked their fiction in the traditional manner. Their language is easy and readable, their base rural. Plot, style and their own individual ways of looking at life, have only made the worlds they have chosen to write about more orderly, more plotted and discrete. As a reader it is easy for me to understand how such life is ordered, because most Indians come from similar rural backgrounds—from towns and villages where life has not undergone much change—where interactions continue to take place without undue intellectualisation of one's purposes and goals. Life matters for these authors above everything else; it is solely their own experience which they have crafted successfully into their art.

Still, what appears to pique us is that such creative literature from the Commonwealth countries has to be appreciated by the Western world before its impact is felt here in India; simply because the West is still the arbiter of such international standards. (The same is the concern with other Third World countries.) But perhaps the Indian novelist is better off than his West Indian or African counterpart in that he does not suffer from the handicap of an absence of tradition. (I am not referring to literary traditions of the novel in English, but to cultural and related traditions in India and Asia.)

One point certainly makes itself felt from a reading of literatures of these very different cultures; and that is, for these three writers at least, a love for the English language stands out—as though it were a gesture of the spirit. They are committed to the language first and above everything else; for somewhere, deep inside them, they feel that *they do not belong to it.* And this is exactly what goes to make their work separate and perhaps exciting. Maybe because of their traditional framework their books have not attracted much critical attention in the West; maybe their writing does not exert appreciable influence in the English-speaking world; and maybe they are intellectually inadequate. . . For this intellectual inadequacy could be the main drawback of the Commonwealth novel, if only it comes about primarily from the lack of modernisation (and all its effects) in such tradition-bound cultures. The plotless, intellectual fiction—Pynchonlike, Grasslike—does not fit into the society in which we are; our realism sounds like an old drum, whose beats we are still incapable of comprehending, and so we are wary of attributing to it unnecessary intellectual dimensions. Baudelaire's restricted postures of the city hold little meanings for us; they seem peripheral to our own needs. In contrast Narayan is real, speaking as he does of the vital processes affecting the common Indian. His words seem to glean a richer yield because they have been nurtured in his silence, away from the 'living' world of the English language. Perhaps isolation has helped a Third World writer that way—and has urged his fiction to take on a relevance beyond the limits of Western critical assessment.

8

A Poet First of All

> "What a mystery this is: thump-thump, thump-thump, and so on all one's life, day and night, summer and winter—the human heart."
>
> —Don Jaime in *The Hive*

When a novel one has read and loved, treasuring the book in secret pleasure for years on end, suddenly bursts forth into the open with the news of its author winning the world's most coveted literary prize, it unquestionably becomes a cause for rejoicing and triumph. Today, the year 1955 is a long way behind us, perhaps a bit of history. But it was that very year I had bought a 35-cent Signet paperback called *The Hive* by an European writer. In Indian currency, I had paid a mere two rupees for the book. The name of the author: Camilo Jose Cela, the Spanish writer who has been awarded this year's Nobel for literature.

Today, *The Hive* remains one of my prized possessions. Published by the New American Library, *The Hive* appeared then in paperback, translated by J.M. Cohen from the original Spanish in consultation with Arturo Barea.

This novel which I have read and reread, reveals a slice of life cut out from the everyday existence of people in the Madrid of 1943. A grim year, no doubt, for the countries of Europe in the grip of war—but, for Spain, more because it was held in the agonising field of a "neutral" dictatorship. Cela, using a uniquely brilliant visual form, more akin to a series of candid camera shots, pulls forth a *tour de force,* a narrative that centres around a sordid, middle-class cafe just off the centre of Madrid.

And with what clarity and compassion does he reveal the pitiful content of the lives of the people who converge on the cafe! We have here all that helps interpret the spiritual crisis of Spain at that time; we feel the greed, fear, frustration, desire, malice, poverty, innocence and tenderness of his characters through small talk and insignificant actions. But, above all, we face the reality of hunger and the element of fear—that is so very much a part of the life we lead in our country today, in the eighties.

I have spoken of *The Hive* by Camilo Jose Cela because, plainly, this was the novel of this great writer which I came across inadvertently in early 1955. And it is a book which describes interconnected, casually-linked people who bear the stigma of the city in which they live. In the individual lives of the people, Cela demonstrates some inner spirit that is still alive, in spite of the aimless, dishonest human actions of an urban world.

Cela's world comes alive strikingly, powerfully, perhaps unlike any other Spanish writer before him. His language even in translation comes out sparse, simple; and yet holds us mute by its penetrating quality. I'd like to quote a small passage at random:

> Martin strokes her face. "You're pale, you look like a bride."
> "Don't be silly."
> "Yes, just like a newly-wed bride."
> Pura turns grave. "Well, I'm not."
> Martin kisses her eyes gently, like a poet of sixteen.
> "For me you are, Pura. Of course you are."

And here's another:

> About half past one or two in the morning, night closes down on the strange heart of the city.
> Thousands of men are sleeping with their arms round their wives, forgetful of the harsh and cruel day that may be lying in wait for them a few hours hence, crouched like a wild cat.
> Hundreds and hundreds of bachelors lapse into the intimate, exalted, utterly refined vice of the solitary.
> And several dozens of girls are hoping—what are they hoping for, O God? Why do YOU let them be thus deceived?— with their minds full of golden dreams...

It is this technique of clipped, short, felt incidents that give the book its form and purpose. Cela himself once said: "I think that today novels can be written—well or badly—only in the way I do it. If I thought the opposite, I should change my profession." Truly a bold and dogmatic statement. And a statement he made in the early fifties.

Moving to and fro between levels of time, Cela ably demonstrates a prose that is repetitive, beating out its own sound and rhythm. Small pools of water into which one can gaze for hours, feel the signs of one's own bitter destiny. A prose that reads like a poem.

Yes, Cela is a poet first of all.

Camilo Jose Cela was born in 1916 in Glicia, Spain's northwestern corner where the Celtic strain is still evident even today. His birthplace was the ancient town of El Padron, called Iria Flavia by the Romans. Before he was twenty (i.e., before the Civil War), Cela wrote lyrics which were obviously influenced by many of the acclaimed younger poets of the thirties. In 1945 he published these poems in a limited edition under the title *Pisando la dudosa luz del dia,* which is a quotation from the great poet Luis de Gongora (and means, simply, "Treading the doubtful light of day.") With these themes like hunger and suffering, Cela started his struggle with life and literature; in his writings later, he was to go on talking of the painful reality of life and the uncertainty of the outer world. His poems are full of the bitterness and pain that go deeper into ourselves despite a seemingly adolescent veneer, with lines such as "damp corpses rotting alone/in the moonless nights...", and which continue to haunt one long after one has read them.

Cela went on to join the Falangist party and fought in General Franco's army during the Civil War. In his prose, one comes across references to the fighting and to an injury he received, but there is no trace of superficial partisanship. In 1942 he published a novel which made him instantly famous throughout the country: *La familia de Pascual Duarte* Pascual Duarte's family). *Pascual Duarte's Family* subsequently appeared in several languages including English, but nowhere did it generate the kind of passionate response it did in Spain.

Realism, in stark and relentless form, finds expression in the story of Pascual Duarte. Narrated in the first person singular by a murderer waiting for his execution, the book is a fluid rendering of the fiery depths of life in which Pascual finds himself. The senseless violence, the brutal poverty depicted in the book are not just aspects of a flat realism, but succeed in bringing out a metaphysical significance through moments of visionary intensity.

Cela's second novel, *Rabellon de Reposo,* was published in 1943. With a theme different from Pascual Duarte, this book plunges into a lyrical sequence of happenings in a sanatorium where the inmates learn to face their own lives without quite overcoming their innermost fears. Cela's third novel entitled *Nuevas adventuras de Lazarillo de Tormes,* relates the adventures of Lazarillo in Spain's unchanging villages where tradition still reigns uppermost.

Sombre colours make up the body of this great Spanish writer's work. Colours that govern human living; the loves and fears, struggles and petty victories of men and women who are able to laugh and weep, live and still hope in the country of Cela's birth. And undoubtedly, much of the material in his books are from Cela's own experiences with people he had encountered.

To me though, *The Hive* is a narrative prose poem, like Cela's other works. Cela's own way of telling a story somehow gives off an aura of remarkable innocence—an innocence that disturbs the reader with its bitter truth, or a form of spirituality that overcomes the loss of human dignity he portrays in his books.

Camilo Jose Cela has been compared, among others, to Hemingway. But maybe he should have been awarded the Nobel Prize for literature years ago, in the fifties when he had already made his mark in the sphere of writing—a writing which served simultaneously as works of art and relevant social document. And, for us Indians, Cela's work has added significance, most of us living as we do today with our own pain-filled poverty and greed, our hate and corruption and senseless violence.

9

The Voice in the Ink

In one of the very last poems Rabindranath Tagore wrote, one comes across once again with those unanswered questions which poetry supposedly tries to give answers to, but fails painfully in the end. Poem after poem done with, made into books and kept away; idea after idea; but the clear order the poet has searched for all his life has gone beyond him. But the poetry has become the long process in man's search to help relate him to the world he lives in, and to civilisation. So, Tagore in a final poem titled *The Unanswered Question* finds himself at a loss for his entire sense of himself and his own work when he asks:

> Faced with the emergence of a new being,
> the first day's sun asked:
> "Who are you?"
> There was no answer.

What sort of question was Tagore dealing with when he wrote this? Surely this was not the manner in which an academic poet today would proceed; there was nothing theoretical here, nothing of theory; simply a subtle attempt toward the painful revelation of a moment of life. I have asked myself often, reading into these lines: what was more alive here, the presence or the illusion? But the answer eludes one. Today, somehow I have come to believe that the poet is neither a philosopher nor a logical being. Nor is he able to connect the value of a poem with the truth of what the poem states. It is feeling alone which seems to me to be the heart of the poem, and it is feeling which starts the poem in the mind of the poet. And perhaps, it is when the act of writing of the poem continues in the poet's mind, that the poet truly learns to feel, moved by feeling itself, eventually being startled by it and experiences the expense of his art—before he gets his sense of life across.

I liked to begin this essay with Tagore simply because there is something of the 'beyond' in many of his apparently unaffected lines. One does not know what poetry is, or what poetry does—but that, like metaphysics, poetry persists in trying to find something of permanence beyond changing appearances, some yet unknown form of a transcendent nature.

Plainly speaking, it is hard to say what these unknown forms we seek through poetry are. And poetry that has been Indian in essence, does take us beyond ourselves, bringing us face to face with that self on the other side, revealing suddenly the mirror opposite of the idea that has gone to make the poem.

Still, it cannot be denied that ideas also exist on their own. One plus one makes two, two and two make four; no matter what we do and howsoever we try to look at this—simply because this is in the mind's own way of seeing things. And we have to agree that nature itself conforms and lets itself be manipulated by the mind. Perhaps the poetic impulse is the intense longing of the poet to get to this inner form which is merely there as a dim, hazy shape in the poet's mind, nothing more. And that is how a poem begins to *become* a poem.

I began this article with poetry that touched the 'beyond' and which has had more relevance for the Indian mind that for other cultures. There is no need to go into this; our own sensibilities have been nurtured on years of tradition when religion was something inseparable from poetry and the arts. And it was only when poets came to regard as their chief function the portrayal of actual contemporary life with all its consequential details that poetry became real, or naked, and simultaneously more difficult to understand.

One of the most significant sayings is that of Santayana, who described himself as "an ignorant man, almost a poet". Like this philosopher, I might presumptuously think the same for myself. Through the years, poets have unwittingly brought themselves under public scrutiny for the nature of their writings, ignorant or not. Time and again one hears the accusation levelled on the poet that he bears a certain responsibility—a responsibility to society for its moral, political and social well-being—and the poet realises how very imperfect this statement is. One need not go into the arguments for and against this. But we have come to recognise universally that poetry has a certain civilising virtue, which provides us in the process a meaningful relationship between life and art.

If we take it that poetry is an activity of the mind, it appears but inevitable that the image of the human being should weave itself into the poem of the working poet. What is the nature and significance of the image of man that finds its way into the poem? What is the image of civilisation expressed in the poems of various poets around the world? How has this image we have encountered in today's poetry affected us, if we are to agree that it has been able to penetrate the centre of our consciousness?

If I approach this topic from my own experiences, there is a danger that my words might seem one-sided and polarised; and yet I feel if I did not do this, I would be guilty of insincerity in my statements. I live in a rural city in coastal Orissa, a place that has always adhered to its rituals and unchanging attitudes, even in the face of change and the intrusion of new technology. As I sit here looking out into the street, feeling the moist wind on my skin, watching the crowds go past immersed in their own hidden desires, some memory or some strange, unsettling wish surfaces to my mind and seems to merge with the susurrus of the breeze in the mango branches in my yeard. A group of lepers shuffling along, with their pitiful whining, disturbs; and the sound of the whip against bullocks' flanks, pulling the heavy load they did not choose, is slow poison. Stray happenings surely; but they tie up a moment of living with others. And I ask myself: what is it that intensifies the merger of such moments to make it into a sort of demand on the poet? Is it because something like acceptance and celebration come together, when two words must fill up the same space in the mind at once, that the tension and passion of the poem happens? Is it that the image and the ceremony must bring about an effect beyond ordinary means—in the poem?

And all because of the boundaries of infinity which the heart appears to possess?

Whatever these moments are, they disturb. And maybe at times when these images urge me to think about this experience, I wish to start the first words of a poem. In a poem titled *The Lost Children of America* written some years ago, the lines came about from those sights which were common in the city of mine in those days. Before me, the high bank of the river, where the smoke of funeral pyres trembles the leaves of the pipals; before me too, a white couple walking hand in hand, apparently visitors from lands beyond our seas. I observe them: shabbily attired, their hair unkempt, they move about barefoot as though they exist in dreams of their own. And it made me wonder why, why is it that these affluent men and women from the West chose to live the poverty-ridden air of India, to make me write this poem and wonder at the truth of life:

> I have no need to ask
> why they come ten thousand miles,
> for though their eyes are open they appear asleep,
> and perhaps they too are men with dreams:
> these men rushing through endless
> supermarket aisles...
>
> appearing like lost children who
> wander bare-eyed
> smelling of incense and living on
> grass and flowers
>
> and loitering around—
> like the dark winds of Asia
> which murmer joylessly in slums but do not answer
> opening their hidden faces
> like lonely picture postcards of unknown lands;
> perhaps some sing, and some others
> chant the mantras of the dead
> with that benign resignation of all children
> or perhaps like victims waiting out
> the relentlessness of time,
> keep watching the skies with terror
> in their gaze.

Difficult to comprehend why people from highly civilised (so-called) societies should endure the malarial, leprous air of

Cuttack streets, I sat down to make *my* sense of this life. But whether I could do it or not in a poem is a different matter. The point is: I wanted to make sense of the life which lay in fragments before me. I was urged to seek answers of myself, testing my feelings by striking them against the fabric of the poem I knew I must write. And so it was that I question not only the subjects of a Western civilisation, but begin to question myself and my own way of life, all the while as I am pitted against odds in my own country—odds I have not been able to unfathom. So, my attempts to embody in my poem the intensities of my own living and the attitudes appropriate to these intensities. But in the end, I suppose, the questions remain; and I fail to understand whether the hippies are *the* lost children or I myself am one of them.

> We gaze at each other in silence, the lost child and I,
> who knows who is playing a joke on whom?
> What can drive me from these mean, sordid alleys
> where I live?
> Who is the one among us, misled by vision,
> more real than real,
> that has filled homes with tremulous ash
> and has brought from hunger unassuaged
> the haunted wood and the hunted myth?

Today, I would say that my poetry suffers from such endless questioning, and also from the cliched subjects of time, death, and the quest which man is after; but such thoughts come out from the meditation on the immediate landscape of my land. I am struck by the poetry of Allen Ginsberg, a poet who has probably lived closer to the limits to the history of his time than any other poet in America, and who has given the image of his society a large-spirited honesty seldom encountered in his fellow poets:

> There is a god
> dying in America
> already created
> in the imagination of man
> made palpable for adoration.

It therefore becomes a natural consequence of the writing of poetry that it should proceed toward a clearer definition of humanity. Maybe to achieve this, the poet tries to redefine his reality in his own terms. It points to the beginning of his fulfilments of living in the act of his writing that he is able to define the role of man on the basis of a more civilised, humane ideology. A fulfilment which accepts the reality of the contribution of every human being to world civilisation, irrespective of race, colour and creed of the peoples of this planet.

The individualness of every human being is of the utmost importance for those who believe in Man. A poet, more than anyone else, is conscious and defines the human being as someone who can give himself upto the essence of all things—who can love, rediscover the essential being, and goes on to tame the instruments of technology for man's needs. Celebration of the elementary qualities of life, such as love, laughter or idleness, by the bond of human brotherhood has been the subject of many of today's great poets, and it would be easy to give examples of these.

Gajanan Madhav Muktibodh, in a poem *To a Formless Void,* once again, in a manner of questioning, brings us much closer to ourselves:

> What a huge existence of what is but non-existent,
> Such a bright light of such a dire darkness.
> People
> Going round and round
> Round and round inside the bubble
> Of the endless void of the shapeless brahman,
> who knows what they seek?
> A lampless journey in the dark of endless nothing
> Is really amazing.

It is poets such as Muktibodh in our own country who have helped us to become intensely aware of our own selves, and to believe in the ultimate dignity and worth of human life. The Korean poet Kim Chi Ha brings forth a similar revelation in a quiet way:

> Peacefully,
> Peaceful as the river at twilight,
> The iris burns over the empty fields.
> Standing there, the sound returns,

of something steadily breaking,
Something that little by little
is falling down.

Here, not only is that poet facing himself, his own life, but his *anti-life*—the other, negative world man is usually blind to.

If poetry makes people more conscious of the complexity and meaning of our experience, it may have an eventual effect upon all action. It appears true that when poetry speaks of the elementary and profound concern of man—and mystery and tragedy of this vital process, this act of living, loving, becoming and dying—it becomes like a pool that gives back our image on the threshold of an experience, like a bright shell in the sea resonant with the accumulated echoes of its past history, which forces us to face the unending change of matter that continues with a troubling beauty after death.

But does much of the poetry written today do this? One does not think so. Certainly, there are competent poems written today in larger numbers than ever, poems which could find a place in any good magazine. But once read, these poems are forgotten. Maybe they do convey a certain idea of feeling, give us a few images, but once read offer little to return to. Maybe this has something to do with the new technology, the habit of ours that is used to seeing a new model of an article every two years—I cannot say. Or maybe it is the effect of the new visual media. But this factor has also entered human relationships in no small measure in recent years, becoming a cause for concern.

Perhaps, to my mind, poetry becomes significant only when the poet makes the reader enter the poem in which the myth-act is present, where the reader has to live the way things *were;* in other words, *where we participate in some myth-journey of man.* It is at such times that we are participating in something both contemporary and ancient, in the story which the poet has built up again in his poem. Here it is that the poem will touch us in our deepest self, because of the myth that is the carrier of the poem.

Edwin Muir said once: "Our minds are possessed by three mysteries: where we came from, where we are going, and since we are not alone, but members of a countless family, how we should live with one another." The truth of this statement cannot be denied. When our poetry reflects this, it goes into those heights that remain for ever. It is this which the poet is supposed to do: to define the symbolic terms of our existience, to show where the human being is in this world we live in. And this, I feel, the poet can do when he does not care for careerism of any sort, when he doesn't write with the view only to get published or win awards—but when he is under the simple necessity to write. Then only, perhaps, poetry will become known as truth.

10

The Moving Horizon: Visiting America

When my young friend, the poet Meena Alexander, asked me if I wanted to wander around Times Square, I was hesitant for no specific reason. It had been drizzling since morning, and it was the evening of October 5, 1995. The streets of New York City were closed to automobile traffic, because the Pope had just been speaking to a large crowd in Central Park. Meena, her husband David Lelyveld, the historian, and I were trying hard to reach their home in East Columbia Street, and it was almost impossible to get a cab. There was no other way left for us but to use the subway, changing trains at 42nd Street. But I find I am digressing from what I am trying to say, My answer to Meena's question was a straight 'No', for I wasn't very much attracted by the wild glitter of Times Square, scenes of which I had seen often in movies throughout my fairly long life. And then, I reasoned to myself, the city was perhaps just as glamorous as another, thinking of the Ginza in Tokyo and Berlin's Kurfurstendamm. I could have been wrong, as I probably have been a number of times about trivial things that have touched my life.

The point is: I did not visit Times Square nor did I walk up and down Broadway, although I spent some time in New York City. My own reasons for this would not satisfy my friends, I realised that. These were never substantial. But I felt smugly ensconsed in my decision.

There is a lot more to the United States of America than either Times Square in New York or the downtown district of

Los Angeles. And I am not trying to romanticise my relationship with the US. I have roamed around Atlanta with my friends, loitered in Pike's Market in Seattle; but *the* city life is what I always seemed to have veered away from. Poetry and politics could perhaps come out from the aroma of coffee in Seattle or from the delightful sight of sea-lions basking on the sun-drenched rocks off La Jolla in California; or the sense of infinite freedom in the faded blue jeans of an often-washed pride; or even in the fact that at least a fifth of all Americans die without warning when the heart gives up its feat to keep on going.

But my America, the northern continent where I was, and which I kept on searching for, in between the many places I encountered through my poetry readings in colleges and universities, was not restricted to superb, acoustically perfect auditoriums and warm, intimate classrooms across this vast country. I realised I was looking out for something else, perhaps for some other levels of living; something that would maybe bring me a feeling of oneness with the country of my own birth, and which I thought I would find in the land's horizon—a horizon that was simply not limited to the curvature of the earth alone. For, like India, the width of North America is somewhat immeasurable, maybe more so; and this gives it a sense of separation from its very own individual, ingrained patterns. I could call it mystery. Einstein had once said that "the most beautiful thing we can experience is the mysterious," and I was on the lookout for something of the kind, which would fill me with a fullness, a sort of union with the unknown. Perhaps a relationship with something like the imaginary line we call the horizon, forever moving away from the specific moments of our living. And I knew it was my traditional Indian mind which pushed me on.

Mystery has sculpted this stoic expanse of America, and there is no denying it. Here I was, patiently witnessing the autumn of 1995. The previous year I had spent two intensely enjoyable weeks on the West Coast, my travels taking me down from the serene San Juan islands into the sprawling, dusty city of San Diego, where the readings I gave of my poetry gave me the longed-for opportunities to travel.

The sight of Mount Rainier will always be a long mystery, a grand moment, bringing in that almost palpable memory that will not go away. I recollect the drunken luminosity of the peak as we passed it by on Delta 255 from Dallas to Seattle; the subsequent shy face of the mountain, shrouded in cloud, as it hung limp from the invisible hands of the sky; and which I never hesitated to watch day after day, with my dear old friend, John Oliver Perry, from the shores of Lake Washington.

There would be people like me, I thought, who would spend much of their time trying to capture the fragile magic of the mountain's colours in their minds alone, and in the end are left merely holding on to the mystery of existence, nothing else. And so I decided to leave behind my cheap 35 everytime I stepped out into the open. My mind seemed enough. The lens would only take me away from what I really saw.

In this piece I should like to touch upon two totally different landscapes of the United States, and which have had a profound effect on my thoughts. Maybe I was not sure of who I was, as I struggled to absorb the two separate images I saw, from the Washington area in the northwest to the southeastern state of South Carolina. Both these landscapes, or worlds, were unfamiliar ones, stranger than the India I knew. It seemed to be an open world, almost a vision of another purer planet, in which one could see, reach up into a higher plane of life. And here, in both these places, strangely enough, the most ordinary elements appeared to take up an intensity of expression that is normally found missing in the Indian landscape.

I could be wrong, yes, but tokens of our awareness remain stuck somewhere in our minds; and the results of silent observation are so deep and abstract that one finds it difficult to talk about them. Any scene, any landscape, of which one becomes an integral part at a specific instant in one's life, is no doubt incomprehensible; there appears only an increased awareness of the self that is linked by an inexplicable silence to an uncertain sense of *not* needing anything in the world.

Perhaps my friend of twenty years, John Perry had seen these sights before; and so he had wanted me to see them. We knew it was not real virgin country. The Washington countryside had innumerable places to be lost in, and I was looking forward excitedly to visiting those; I was eager especially for isolated sanctuaries away from the crowded shores of the lake, where one could just feel the warm afternoon summer sun stream down through the sparse spaces it could perhaps find between the trees, to dapple the forest floor layered by sorrel and fern and moss.

We parked the dusty old car somewhere in a small clearing where the road seemed to end. Somehow my interest in trees had remained unchanged since my childhood. Or, more truthfully, it had grown through the years, and one of my deeprooted urges had always been to see these giant sequoias and redwoods I had read so much about.

The forest footpath opened before us into a rich depth of landscape I had only imagined in my rarest dreams. Denny Creek is a dream place of a prophecy: of a knowing and a not knowing. Of knowing through our eyes the stretch of reverent forest as we slowly climbed the narrow twisted path close to the mountain stream on our left. And of not knowing the silence of sunlight and shadow that seemed to gain a measure of spirituality from unknown, unfound preserves of history and myth.

I remember we kept our voices low. Even our careful light footfalls appeared to defile the purity of the forest. On all sides of us the forest grew; giant trees of sequoia, fir and redwood with their myriad networks of branches. The sun had been blanketed. There was simply a subdued glow, that appeared to emanate from the trees themselves. Wherever I looked, I saw both forest and stream transformed by an inner energy, a pleasing inner light. And through this extraordinary quiet radiance, I could sense an amorphous, piercing silence—the silence of the forest around Denny Creek.

I drew near a great sequoia. My mind and body both wanted to be close to it, to feel its largeness, its silence and magic. Instinctively, my eyes travelled upward. My gaze could only take in a mere thirty feet of the huge trunk before it got lost in the maze of intertwining limbs of other trees. I touched the coarse, deeply-furrowed bark, marvelling at the reservoir of its age, the stillness of its massive body. I let my own body reach out toward this other one, stretching pathetically against it, feeling time, and the brief flash of understanding of what a light year was. All my knowledge of Physics had not made me comprehend time and the images of constancy to which we involuntarily turn. Here I was, face to face, against a door. An unknown door of awareness, which I felt and realised I could never enter.

We followed the forest footpath higher and higher. Trees were everywhere, both living and dead, many fallen arbitrarily on the forest floor and across the gurgling stream. The appearance of these trees was the most important fact about them. Through the forest canopy the giants seemed to breathe their sap into us, offering up their breaths so we could share in part the silent incantations of the years they had lived. Those giant trees belonged to a different world, and I felt the metaphor for time dance away out of reach of our meagre human understanding.

So I found that a part of the American northwest was built of silence. The place of dream was the forest of ancient redwood and sequoia, and the dark forest floor of moss and lichen, and also where stranger plants wander over the massive trunks softening the rough bark with exquisite flowers. But this quietness was very different. This quietness was of the mystery of life itself. Something I had not experienced in the jagged, masculine ranges of the Rockies in Colorado I had visited two weeks before, or in the unending fields of corn in the midwest. It was not only there in the roof of leaf and branch high overhead, it took root in the soil of the forest floor, among the blend of twigs, needles, fir cones and general forest litter. And this silence came from the forest itself, standing, breathing, listening to the wind.

The American South holds a remarkable geological fragility. It might be hard for some to sympathise with this view of mine; but I feel that the landscape of the South holds more than the history associated with these places in the southern states. Whether it is Tennessee, or the two Carolinas, one encounters an unaccountable difficulty in judging the landscape; and it makes one ask oneself: Is it because of the history which is linked inexorably with it, or because of the attitudes of generations of Americans toward its own history? It is not right that I interfere with movements beyond apparent reality. Here I was only a visitor who seemed to take sustenance from what I saw and felt. And I sensed an extraordinary detachment in *the* world of the South. But I would only like to talk about a landscape I "discovered" near the small university campus of South Carolina State University in Orangeberg—a place which many visitors would not see.

Was it an indifference to the movement of the blood that flowed in my own veins I found in this small southern town? Or was it the stirring of something sublime, that is the material for poetry and for an awareness of human understanding? I do not know. But I came face to face with a time when I felt I had never loved the strange part of myself more.

October was nearing its end. The ground was beginning to show its litter of leaves. A number of cotton fields we had passed by on our way from the university town of Laurinburg in North Carolina had already been sheared, and the few remaining ones would soon lose their coherent spread of white, as the cotton would be shipped to various mills. Something is always stirring in these old fields, for they seem to sing in the mellow sun as the old cotton-pickers used to do. There is so much happening in these open spaces; it is there in the air when someone is intently listening. And each minute one spends here is memory; and history that goes unnoticed as we don't bother to know something of the memory of old cotton fields.

My young friend Bijoy and I took time off one afternoon to walk along the banks of the river that ran through Orangeberg. Bijoy is young, years younger; but we have always thought alike, seen and loved things alike. He had been living in the US for about a decade now and taught at the SCSU. But I was a pilgrim. Perhaps just like everybody else who visits the US. In front of me was a river, the likes of which I had not seen elsewhere. The River Edisto. Fringed by maples and cottonwoods, the waters of the Edisto looked dark and foreboding. The currents were swift; leaves and small twigs were swept downstream as though with some dark, strange purpose. I watched the scene before me with potential unease. Anyone reading this memoir would surely ask: Why has someone to write about this common-looking, black stream of a river like the Edisto, instead of the Potomac or the Mississippi? Once again, I have no answers for that. The River Edisto is unlike any other river I have seen; centuries stare back at you with black, haughty eyes.

It is a spiritual river. I can't say what I exactly mean by that; but to be there, walking or simply sitting on the bank, seems to bring in a physical sensation in one. I felt as though I were inside some cold subterranean cave in the deeps of some sea. Maybe I tended to look inward, as a silence began to build inside me, and there was a consequent absence of thought.

And yet the sinister atmosphere surrounding the river was broken by slivers of sunlight that came down through the trees to be trapped by the clear water of the Edisto. One could see the water striders flitting past on the surface, their frail shadows visible at times on the shallow river floor near the bank where I sat. Beyond us, were vague and anonymous depths; the water was the colour of soul. On both banks of the river, the trees and the swampy soil mingle with one another when the river overflows; with the decidedly strange sense of things one can never see but feel. And then I notice the queer roots of those trees jutting out of the water like leprous, mutilated human limbs I have often encountered in my own country, startling me.

Here, by the Edisto, I should not have been surprised to find a Pee Wee Indian at my elbow, smoking his clay pipe; nor to see a Southern officer, sitting on his horse, silently watching me from the other bank. For here, time has stood still; and perhaps one feels that time will bury us when we are still alive. Walking the river bank is an uneasy experience. To add to the queerness of the scene, is the weird ash-coloured weed known as Spanish Moss, that grows in different lengths and hangs from the branches of the trees lining the river. Neither Spanish nor a moss, the wavy, light brushes of the growth appear ghostly against the black Edisto, and add to the mysteries of natural growths about which I seem to know less. It's only that such things make us talk in whispers when we are here, nothing else.

So the South will always have its strange fascination for me, because of things I have not been able to understand. I heard a saying during my travels around North America that *even* a white man can listen closely and understand how the drum *is* the Indian-American's heart. And here I was, another Indian from another land, and un-white. But there were spirits of the departed that one could sense if one sat long enough and listened to the air. Maybe this is what the spirit does to one, and it does not matter where the spirit comes from.

At the end I feel, if I have not spoken deliberately about the sprawling gilt-and-chromium cities I have visited, it is because of the sameness of their machine-like faces; but more because of the absence of that need in me to become invisible, which I experienced profoundly in the dark area of the Low Country.

There appear to be miracles happening around the world, like walking on water; but for me these are but symbols of the power of silence. America's magical showpieces lie deep inside the country's womb; they leave no signs in the accessible city landscape. But the doors are there, for anyone who chooses to open them: to stand to brightness, and wonder at the forest rising pine-scented into the night; or to feel the strange power of a black, silent river seep into one's bones.

And so I speak to myself as to a child once again. I don't know if *that* is enough. Or if I am born now, again.

11

Acceptance Speech on Receiving the Sahitya Akademi Award for *Relationship*, 1981

I am grateful to the Sahitya Akademi for the honour it has thought fit to confer upon me. I do not know how far I deserve it; and today as I think of other writers who have not received the Award, the Akademi's selection makes me accept it only with the utmost humility.

It is not for me to deliver a speech. Inept at any form of oratory, I am at a loss for words. I can merely thank so distinguished an assembly for its recognition to poetry written in the English language in our country. I am quite aware of having learned something from my predecessors and contemporaries, from each one writing in the many languages of India—and a little of which has been rendered into English for me to know. I am aware of my debt to poets and writers of my state, Orissa; the debt to the poets of lands beyond my own, and writing in tongues totally foreign to me, but whose innermost feelings have quietly seeped into my own work through the medium of English.

To Orissa, to this land in which my roots lie and lies my past, and in which lies my beginning and my end, where the wind keens over the great grief of the River Daya and where the waves of the Bay of Bengal fail to reach out today to the twilight soul of Konarka, I acknowledge my debt and my relationship.

Once again, I thank you.

12

Face to Face with the Contemporary Poem

Once again, I feel it would be audacious to speak about the poetry I write, plainly because I realise that my years have *not* been spent learning the makings of verse, its art and craft, studying the procedures which distinguish the good poem from the bad — in academic centres. In other words, I admit that I am not an academic, and that I did not read any poetry until I started writing it myself (which was rather late in life), except for a dozen poems in my last year at school, the usual which ranged from Keats to Wordsworth. Therefore, whatever I might have to say will only be a limited voice, because of my lack of proper critical approach, but certainly will move toward an honest realisation of my innermost convictions. Secondly, and this is what seems of primary importance to me, is that, as a practising poet my job is to write poems, and not to go about exploiting the suggestions of my verse.

I would say *conscience* matters, because what else is the poet responsible to? Nothing else is as consequential as this 'inner thing' to him, this secret root of his being, and which acts as the hidden code behind his writing. A poet is, perhaps, only right when he says in his poem what he has actually known. This appears as the only relevant truth: that one's experience in the world is the raw material from which the poem is made. Usually writers do rely on their individual, personal experiences—on those things that can be seen and heard, touched and trapped by their senses, which threaten their ephemeral existence—to produce their own poems. For, it is then that the poem becomes the only reliable authority to which one can turn to if one is to recognise the shapes and movements of life.

I do not, however, wish to discuss if such an experience is appropriate to the making of a memorable poem; and, that besides the central experience nothing else matters. For I am not going into the process or build-up of a *significant* poem; it is simply that a poem becomes a testament on the page, a testament of the poet's ability towards life, and his own way of breaking forth an experience into a responsibility which cannot be dismissed. William Carlos Williams said it, without jargon, "Because it's there to be written," in the manner of the Everest mountaineer who lost his life years ago, "Because it's there." And it is hard, most of the time, to ascribe any rationale for the writing of a particular poem; it's just that a part of the mystery of one's self comes out, perhaps in the manner of a truth, or a decorative gesture, or in virtuous attire—a reality that endures that specific instant of thought. A good number of my own poems have their roots in day-to-day common experiences (I should like to cite "The Report Card", "The Abandoned British Graveyard at Balasore, India", and "Grandfather" as examples, and these have probably turned out to be "ordinary" poems.) I shall label them "insignificant" in the broader context of poetry because the experiences from which they originate are trivial ones; therefore, to the general reader insignificant. I do not (here) put forward any pretensions that any one of those three mentioned above be called memorable or signficant. Perhaps thought, language, imagery and metaphor are all present in the poems—but then do these factors only qualify for a poem's greatness? Not the honesty and meaning of a poem? And should a great poem be the only grand occasion for taking stock of a society's artistic capabilities?

It is my intention here not to refer to this unity of fullness in a poem (and how a great poem lets us embark on a sort of journey or voyage through symbols and allusions to encompass the human condition), but to deal with any poem or verse that qualifies enough to be called poetry, arising out of the commonplace experiences of our time. In such a poem the experience emerges as the core around which the whole writing-structure is built. And yet, how strange it is that the act of making or writing the poem itself becomes a *full* experience! I am afraid it is not in my thinking to explain this apparent discrepancy; I see it as a question one has to live with. But no one can deny that the act of writing any poem, significant or small, is only the poet's concern, the poet's secret deal. And this writing of it is a lonely and difficult affair. The poet himself cannot pretend to know how the poem will progress, and *how the poem wants him, to be.* For it is only the poet who finds himself at last, after the word has been written down. His private life does not remain a private thing for too long, and as the poem imposes itself upon the poet in the process of his writing, the poet is unable to tell whether he has suffered his realisation of what he is.

It appears correct for me to insist that the manner of writing a poem is a painful one. This is true also of today's poem, the contemporary poem, in which according to popular comment, meaning is neither clear nor explicit—and to extract a statement or understanding from the poem becomes "difficult". When the "confessional" poetry of the sixties in America (markedly) gave way to a new "surrealism", it evidenced a new ambiguity—not what the lay or common reader could follow, not something he had come to regard as poetry through the years. Generally speaking, today's poem utilises a number of images and symbols to form a whole, leaving the reader to extricate himself with the valid meaning or argument from them. Thus the reader is left to find out his own meaning from the poem; this, I admit painfully, is true of much of the poetry I have written. If, contemporary life is no longer what it was, say, twenty-five years back, can one expect the same content, the same form, the same substance from contemporary poems? And yet poets are expected to create a unifying sense from contemporary existence, not to portray or reflect the fragments and pieces they encounter in their day-to-day living.

How far a poet is able to relate to the reader thus becomes the crucial thing; a seemingly obscure poem does, in its content, contain the hidden voice for its ultimate understanding. For even though the poetry of the past two decades or so has become a very personal matter (as evidenced by the poems in anthologies and periodicals, and which don't concern many people), a true poem should make the reader feel how the poem *wants* him, should build that relationship by making him feel and not merely tell him a certain thing. Certainly, therefore, the poet faces a difficult task. But, besides this, the reader (whether he be layman or critic) is responsible; and he should be aware, of the poet's predicament in order that communication between them is possible.

This feeling or *wanting* of the reader to the poem can be poor or good; often, the reader reads the opening (first/second) lines of the poem and then ditches it for another thing—another literary form, like a story or essay. Why does this happen? Is it because the first two lines of the poem are trite and uninviting, or is it that they remind the reader of the refuse of a greater poet he has read and admired? Is it because our existence today has corrupted our normally-open instincts by the excessive interruption of politics so that the ordinary reader is turned off simply by the sight of a poem? Or has our culture become so "popular" that serious poetry has lost its readers for good? Or, coming to the poem itself—and this from a writer's viewpoint—*is* the contemporary poem too poor to evoke a response in the reader?

All poems cannot be good, and powerful, and, often, the ordinary reader is confronted by a poorly-written poem. He is justified thus to deride the state of contemporary poetry in our day. This is a general statement and covers both Indian writing and poetry being written in other countries as well. And this is not the reader's fault. The relation between a poem and reader is a reversible process, a two-way affair. And how an individual poem is able to put forth its experience so as to touch the reader is important and decisive: this experience might (i) reach the reader almost immediately, spontaneously—in the manner of electric charge passing through a good conductor such as copper or iron, (ii) reach the reader with difficulty, slowly, under great stress, like that of charge passing through a bad conductor like glass, or (iii) not be able to pass or communicate at all, as though there was a break or gap between them.

It becomes safe to conclude that the capacity or power for conducting the essential experience of the poem will primarily depend upon the poem itself—on the poem's design. Together with this, lies the responsibility of the experience in the poem perhaps to its awe, to its delight, and to its hopes and fears. And no one can refute the fact that experience is an ambiguous thing, difficult to explain—an unknown quantity (x) that the poet wishes to give concrete form to in a poem, in order that it may reach out for another unknown.

I feel therefore, that the reader's experience is a necessary one, for the reader to be *wanted* by the poem, to share the poem's mystery and its content in full. Otherwise the reader's response becomes a partial, superficial one. Also, confront here an encounter between two separate cultures, belonging to the poet and to the reader, because the poem is never addressed to a single, homogeneous audience. For instance, a reader from a Westernised or technologically advanced culture (usually considered a superior culture) will come upon a number of obstacles in reading the poems of one who is reconciled and (apparently) content with backward conditions at home. I am aware of this groping when a city reader reads my work. Taking my poems in the last two books, *A Rain of Rites* and *Waiting*, where the poems deal with Orissa—an area where I have lived almost all my life—I meet the befuddled reader/critic. The poems are woven from the unchanging ways of life in the temple cities of Puri and Bhubaneswar, with the unquestionable rituals of a predominantly agricultural society. How then, could a reader living outside Orissa react to such a poetry abounding in local detail? How could he react fully to the poems, feel himself *wanted* by them? What reactions could one, then, expect from a non-Indian reader? And how can one blame the reader (or reviewer) for being blind to some of the important aspects of this verse? And this does explain somewhat the state of criticism of Western readers toward Indian poetry.

As I remarked earlier, the contemporary poem stems from a confused and loose earth, quite unlike the one our forefathers lived in. Values have changed considerably through the years;

indeed, so much so that they have come to resemble abnormalities. The sensibility of an earlier century is not here any longer, not here any more to push man into the continuum of nature, to establish him close to the banyan-bark and to the leaf, to the owl's hoot and the mantiss, to those symbols which enabled him to reach beyond himself. Will it be a cruel thing to say that the reader of today's poem needs an external set of antennae to feel his own knowing? To feel pain and sadness and infinitude? Or, has the taste for the poem been robbed by a new, technologically-oriented culture? A culture which is excited, nourished by flamboyant media—by a system of super advertisement that strips symbols and words of their time-proved meanings?

Perhaps the pedantic, intellectual poetry which many significant twentieth-century poets wrote was responsible for this loss of popular appeal (the poetry suffered from a loss of coherence); it would be easy to name these modernist poets—poets who had among their audience other poets and academics; and this probably led to their poetry being confined to the English departments of universities. Outside the campuses their poetry failed, basically because of a difference in outlook between poet and reader. And this still ails the state of poetry today.

The medium being language in poetry, language makes greater demands on the artist. An almost pure art like music is capable of creating an immediate response. Musical sounds are not ordinarily used for other purposes. Visual arts like painting and sculpture are also in an advantageous position, because the pictorial element can at once relate to the viewer—maybe not on the truly aesthetic plane, but on some other. Poetry becomes the most difficult of the arts because it operates on language; and language is used to relate, to communicate with the world every moment of our lives. Thus, for language to be successful in poetry, it must be made to work for the poet, with an additional boost. In other words, poetry has to make use of *language plus*—that is, a human language (not utilitarian like science or day-to-day speech), a language of over-and-above noumenal concerns.

Strange that everyone feels a poem is easy to make. For on the page it appears exceptionally neat and ordered—perhaps resembling a convenient piece of architecture. Therefore all kinds of people find it simple to talk about it, to dismiss it lightly, but not any other art form such as painting or sculpture. I am at a loss to know what sort of pleasure poetry gives. Is it of a different kind, bringing a refined delight? Or is it capable of producing a reverse, numbing effect on the mind?

When I reread the poetry I have written, I find many of the poems confused, made up of abstractions which fail to connect with the reader. (This is especially true of my earlier work.) For every poem one makes is a step forward, a process—just as thought itself is a process—and gradually the language changes, expanding and contracting as time passes by, the words curve and straighten and vibrate with the silence around and inside the imagination. How unfortunate that, unlike a scientist, one is unable to wash out all the errors, the absurd and poor arguments, when he arrives at a fruitful conclusion! But with verse, each poem one leaves behind becomes witness to a crude experience of the poet, becomes an anguish that he cannot overcome, on the way to a continued growth as a writer. One discovers that the old ideas still continue to condition his emotions. So I am very tentative in admitting to myself that I am a poet. Governed as one is, as I am by the unconscious—which in more ways than one acts like a power-generator, behaving like a god—I would be satisfied if I can reveal a consciousness in my writing in agreement with today's realities.

To conclude, the pertinent question: how many would read the poems I've written? Perhaps twenty, or thirty people at the most. It won't be an understatement when I say that in Cuttack, my home town, a small number (say, about ten) read my poems, discuss them, and walk home perhaps with unfinished feelings. They are all youngsters in their late teens or early twenties. I keep on asking myself: Do they like what they read? Are they really interested? Have the poems been able to expand their moments of sensibility in some way? I don't have any answers. And here I have to admit truthfully that the college where I've been teaching all these years does not have a single collection of my poetry on the library shelves. Doesn't this confirm my fears that my readership is severely limited? Isn't it right that I assume that nobody cares a damn about the stuff I write?

It is not always possible to make meaning and sense of life, and poets are expected to do just that. Auden wasn't uncomfortable when he said "poetry makes nothing happen." And yet, when one looks at a poem on a page, he faces a response to a part of himself: the poem looks back at him: it is there, taking care of itself, and perhaps that's enough.

13

Our Escapist Art

If one might, quite reasonably, suppose that our concern with life and whatever it is that gives substance to life, is culture—then it would be right *not* to categorise culture. There is no doubt that life and its assumptions are greatly different as one proceeds from place to place: for instance, it is never the same at Mumbai as it is at Madurai, at New Delhi as it is in the tiny village of Paraja Limika in Orissa's Koraput district. Immense differences truly, when one compares the processes of living between the Ramaswamy family in Madurai and the Mundas of rural Sambalpur. What I should like to stress is: that the term "Indian culture" becomes meaningless, simply because our songs and our anticipations are very, very separate from one another.

It would consequntly sound false when terms such as "elitist" and "proletarian" are applied to our notion of culture. One could talk of the elite being superior, individualistic; but definitely not linked to an abundance of material wealth. Does the acquisition of an exquisite Madhubani in a rich man's house make the owner elitist because it is in vogue to collect such objects? Never. You cannot make folk or ethnic art "elitist" merely by placing such pieces in affluent living rooms of our country.

Personally, I don't like the word "elitist". Nor the word "proletarian". These are stupid words indeed, in the context of our talk about culture. Can beauty, for example, be classed as "elitist" or "proletarian"? And culture, like beauty perhaps, is a subtle thing, very much like nature which we experience around us. But taste; it could certainly be individualistic "elitist".

Often I have watched Adivasi women walk past me in rural Orissa, draped in Odissi sarees (in shorter lengths though) which are so much the rage these days. And I ask myself: Doesn't that traditional saree suit the Kondh woman better? Doesn't it look out of place on the body of the Doordarshan announcer?

A remark made by the late Prof A.L. Basham at a seminar at the Australian National University in Canberra some years ago comes to my mind. Basham commented on the highly popular Hindi novels of Gulshan Nanda and said that it was literature because it appealed to a vast number of readers.

Similarly, in the realm of cinema, it wouldn't be correct to dismiss the films of Prakash Mehra or Manmohan Desai as commonplace. We could say the same of film songs or of the framed pictures of our gods and of calendars.

The fact remains that our art, which is deeply rooted in religion, is escapist. We, as a people, like to live in a world of fancy, of dream. And, if we have become escapists, our rulers and governments are responsible for these attitudes. What does the word "culture" matter to our huge, illiterate population of about 500 million—many of whom don't even have their basic daily sustenance?

But who am I to talk of such things when I write in English? Or write a poem which ten people read and understand?

Let us not make art into a deity, into an icon of worship.

14

An August Day in 1942

August, a time of rain, when the earth is already wet with the continual showers of the first monsoon and is blossoming with newborn things; a time of clouds too, falling apart on lotus leaves in village pools. A flame of rain, when golden orioles rush through the mango groves by the river, giving vent to their melodious calls, as though greeting man and nature alike with their songs. A time when all life seems to renew itself in its own mysterious manner.

Yes, August is a time for renewal, especially for us in India. As I write this, my thoughts inevitably go back to the past, years back, when a hand-spun cotton tricoloured flag began to flutter triumphantly in our minds, as it ushered in a new era of hope and joy; when dreams began to take shape in that darkness foreign rulers were leaving behind. It was a time to be ecstatic, and to be proud of the pulsing of our blood; blood that began shaping the people we were and the people we would later become.

But I am speaking of a day when I was a mere boy of thirteen newly out from school, and had just been admitted into the first year science class of this premier college of Orissa. Ravenshaw College in Cuttack seemed a towering edifice in those days, with vain-looking buildings, exquisitely laid-out lawns lush with grass, clay tennis courts, and a pair of quaint old cannons pointing at a past most of us had forgotten, and which only served to conjure up images of wounds and defeat when one thought of them.

Fifty years have passed by since the auspicious conches heralded a new epoch, their deep sounds dimpling the midnight-face of this country on the 15th of August. But my mind goes back five years further, to another cloudy morning in August. It was a fine day, and we had just settled down, all one hundred and twenty-eight of us to the droning of our English professor. The lecture theatre in which we were seated was a fairly large one; was I in one of the front rows, I ask myself today? But I remember the text being discussed—it was the poem, *Atlanta's Race*. Our professor had reached the point where Atlanta had stooped down to retrieve her second apple as she raced against her charming rival, who was slowly and steadily overtaking her. But my restless mind had wandered off as it always did, somewhere out of the room, beyond the wide windows, into the clouds and to the realm of dreams—when a sudden commotion outside brought me back to reality.

A small group of students soon collected at the door of the lecture theatre. Shouts of *Inquilab Zindabad* and *Britishers, Quit India* reverberated along the corridor. The professor looked nonplussed and stopped midway through a sentence. All eyes inside were riveted on the excited group of students outside who were now urging us to leave the classroom. And then, from inside the hall, someone's lone voice started echoing *Quit India*. A strange elation gripped all of us. These were things I could not completely understand, and yet the voices of my fellow students quickened my blood. One by one, and then in a mad rush, all of us left the lecture theatre. Slowly we gathered with the others in the tennis courts outside the college building.

It was almost noon by then. An hour had passed by since the time we had left our class. The crowd of students had swelled with the leaders of the union giving vent to their fiery words against the British government. Mahatma Gandhi, I heard the words, Mahatma Gandhi. He was a mere name to me then, and that was all I knew. And that Gandhi was a voice that was unafraid to speak out against injustice. It was difficult to judge what was happening all over the country, but I acutely realised that something had begun. The sky seemed to redden as I looked. Perhaps the hour had come. And we were in it, somehow. Something I had to be in too, alongwith my fellow students.

I was only thirteen. My fourteenth birthday was still some way off, and frankly I was a little nervous about the happenings around. The events of that day went too fast for me to recollect them with coherence. But I remember all of us walked round the college building, shouting slogans. By the time we had made a complete circle, voices had risen, shouts and slogans had grown more aggressive. What did I understand then as to how the British would be driven out of India? I didn't. As I turned the corner, moving along with the others, I saw a column of smoke rising out of the administrative offices. How had the building caught fire? Was it one of us who had done it? I felt isolated. The sight of the fire made me more jumpy. Thoughts of being arrested by the police entered my mind. I pushed myself deeper into the mass of students and felt secure in the enveloping crowd.

In a few minutes I found we were walking out of the main gates of our college. A few women students were leading the procession; somehow I was reassured seeing them with me. Undoubtedly an excitement possessed us; the tricolour with its *charkha* flapping in the wind, the shouts of fellow compatriots, and my indisciplined feet trailing behind. I watched with unconcealed pride the sight of onlookers happily staring at us from distant windows and shop-windows, and sensed the surge of a wild joy inside me. And yet, the fear persisted—of the unknown, of what was going to happen ahead, as we went on shaking our small hands at a vast and inconceivable sky.

But perhaps there was no real reason to worry as we walked down the busy Ranihat street and entered the spacious compound of the Prince of Wales Medical School. True we were out fighting for a national cause, proud to be hitting out at our rulers, the British—but we looked at one another and didn't feel hopeful. The number of students increased as we entered the hospital yard; students of the medical school had joined us. We were somewhat jubilant. And I watched as the student leaders shouted provocative slogans, and guided us into the large open space of the hospital yard.

I can clearly recollect the formation we made. All of us were grouped roughly in rows, and there were about a thousand of us. In the front row were the women students, about seven of them. I was somewhere down behind, perhaps in the tenth row.

But what happened then, escapes my mind. I remember I couldn't see over the heads of those in front of me, short as I was. My books were clutched in my hand. A sudden uproar in the front row made me look up. Two jeeps and a pick-up van had driven in meanwhile and were parked to one side.

Without any reason, I began feeling inexpressibly lonely. I didn't seem to know the students who stood there around me. And I didn't seem to remember what I was doing there, away from my college where I should have been attending classes. Somehow I had become aware of myself in a way I had never quite experienced before.

The pink-faced English sergeant with his military-looking moustache loomed formidably as he alighted from his jeep and walked towards the massed group of students. Behind him, falling into line were a number of policemen, wielding metal-tipped lathis. As I watched on apprehensively, I heard the sergeant shout at us to disperse. The air grew tense. We fidgeted uneasily in our places. The student leaders cautioned us not to move. Events happened too swiftly then for me to comprehend. I noticed that the women students who were leading the procession had moved off to one side and were engaged in an argument with the sergeant. A quiet descended over the whole gathering. Abruptly then, the word *Charge!* resounded through the air.

There was turmoil all around as the policemen started striking ferociously at the demonstrators in the first few rows with their lathis. The students scattered and fled. Perhaps never until that moment in my life had I known what fear was. It was each one for himself. I ran as fast as my spindly legs could carry me, across the hospital compound to my left and reached the old boundary wall. In no time I had scaled it and was on the other side—landing in someone's house. The events of that fateful afternoon are hazy still. That I had trespassed into private property seemed immaterial to me. Just as the idea of ousting the British became of no consequence at that moment. Only the thought of escaping from that place was uppermost in my mind. I turned round and saw a few policemen still chasing some students back against the hospital buildings.

Fear was behind me. I stood mournfully for a second and began walking swiftly toward a veranda of another nearby house. I hid myself behind a wall for some time. My heart was thumping madly against my chest as I waited to regain my breath. From that distance I could see books, papers and shoes lying all over the hospital grounds. The wounded were being picked up and taken to an ambulance. And I felt myself lucky to have escaped the wrath of the British colonials.

Perhaps until that moment I hadn't really cared about what was happening. The delirium of the entire movement had swept me along. Now I felt alone once again, a thirteen-year-old unsure of happenings around him.

My books were lost. My sandals too. My shirt and shorts were dishevelled and dirty. And my bicycle was parked in the college bicycle-shed almost two kilometres away from where I was. I knew I had to retrieve my bicycle first and then wind my way home.

I must have waited a long while before I plucked up enough courage to retrace my steps through the back lanes and cross the Ranihat Canal bridge leading to Ravenshaw College. Curiously, the streets wore a deserted look. The sun was setting by the time I staggered into the shed barefoot and unlocked my bicycle from among those still there. Four hours had passed by since we had marched from the college, and home was still a five-kilometre ride away.

Whether this experience, in its loneliness, had anything to do with the long, slow realization that I would always be somehow alone in my life, I do not know. But it brought me closer to the truths I learnt later, truths other than what I had seen and experienced that day.

I cycled past the darkening trees and the low-lying marshland in the deepening twilight. Crows were settling down raucously to the night. My feet were sore and I was slowly becoming aware of a dull throbbing in my head, the colour of blood.

The oil lanterns were already lit when I opened the gate and literally fell through the front door in my eagerness to reach home. I had expected it to be locked. Mother usually bolted it before it grew dark. But strangely the door was open today.

A familiar shape detached itself from the clump of pale yellow light on the veranda and came toward me. It was difficult to see his features in the surrounding darkness. In sheer surprise I watched my father's comforting form reach out and envelop my exhausted self.

"Where were you, my son? I went out and looked for you everywhere I could."

Father had taken a bus from his place of work and travelled to Cuttack at once when he had heard of the incidents of that afternoon in the college.

But it took me years to realise the truth of that precise moment in my life. I have forgotten the cruel Sergeant Hargreaves, but not that face in the darkness of our home. Only years later, when my three-year-old son was lost at dusk on the seemingly endless sands at Puri, did I see that face of his, rich and burning with care and anxiety.

And I knew then what my father had felt that long-ago evening of August 1942.

15

Publishing in India: An Overview

Publishing has always been an affirmation, through the exercise of the creative power of the writer, of the culture to which the writer belongs. In India, however, this process seems to be only partial, because of the insurmountable barrier between the work of the creative writer and the passive illiterate millions. There arises also the question: which culture, which Indianness does any one writer represent?

The vastness of the subcontinent, with its varied regions and their peoples' many different languages and dialects, belies the suggestion of a single Indian vision. The post-Independence breaking up of the country into linguistic regions brought added fervour among writers to pursue their ideas in their respective languages. Publishing then stepped up. Today, books and periodicals continue to appear more and more in the regional languages—from Marathi in the west to Bengali in the east, from Dogri up north to Tamil in the south. Yet strangely enough, in spite of a growing antagonism toward the use of English, noticeable in the Hindi-speaking belt in the country, more books are published in English annually than in all the regional languages taken together.

Indian writing has been inhibited by long-standing traditions, in both poetry and prose, discernible in much of the literature published in the regional languages. In a country which still adheres passionately to the ritualistic singing and enactment of verses from the epic poems of as long as four thousand years ago, and where Hinduism is a way of life, publications continue to appear on the same old religious themes—sustaining, perhaps, but a form of lowest common multiple. Manipulative adaptations of parts of the cultural heritage also prove a continual temptation in India, both in the realm of publishing and in other contemporary media.

The last few decades have, however, witnessed some exploration of issues more relevant to contemporary life. Books have been published on the problems of poverty and caste, of sexuality and the subjugation of women. I recently read a poignant account of amniocentesis, where the writer cited a prenatal survey for sex determination in Delhi. 7,999 of the 8,000 abortions were of female foetuses. Such frankness would have been unthinkable in Indian publishing ten years back.

Certain kinds of publishing are difficult today, if not impossible. For instance, it isn't easy to find a publisher for serious poetry, and this has made writers turn to the West for publication. Three of my own poetry collections first appeared in the United States; and my book which received the Sahitya Akademi (India's National Academy of Letters) Award was first brought out by an American publisher. This is not an isolated instance.

I suppose that similar problems exist in publishing everywhere. But in a developing country like ours, with the added hazards of growing regional chauvinism and a huge, poor and illiterate population, it is slowly becoming apparent that regional cultures are moving away from one another. Meanwhile, the mechanisms of power are responsible for reducing us to a sad passivity. To listen to speeches, most of all to watch television (a novelty in India), are becoming forms of hypnosis. Are we witnessing the death of literature in some way? Probably not. But the proper function of publishing in India is not merely to improve rhetoric, let alone to cultivate the *mantra* of a past culture.

16

Translating from Oriya: An Approach

Translation, especially from the various Indian languages, is a relatively recent phenomenon. I will confine myself in this piece to some of the problems arising out of translation from Oriya to English; and I believe that these can apply to almost all the languages in India. To all accounts, very little work pertaining to translation has been done in the pre-independence period. Whatever we find today was probably done by a few persons who knew English (the recipient language) but were inept in the subtleties of the Oriya language—thereby producing translations which read unevenly and possess a stilted and forced quality throughout.

My area of translation has been mainly confined to Oriya poetry, both contemporary and ancient. But of the latter I have, to date, done fairly little. This is because of reasons I will discuss later in the article. I should like to believe that I am an original poet myself—primarily writing in English—and hence the translations I have undertaken (I am not ashamed to confess) are secondary to me. In other words, I would perhaps take up translations of Oriya poetry into English only when I come up against a sort of blank wall in my own work, that is, when I face a "no writing" period at times. And this, one is apt to suppose, happens to most writers (mainly poets perhaps) who consider translation a secondrate activity, and will only take it up as an exercise when they feel creatively deadened at certain stages of their careers.

The next point which arises is this: if translation is considered to be an "inferior" form of activity, will a practising writer or poet engaged in the act of translation ever be able to devote his *entire* effort to it? Will he pursue this process of translation with the same amount of verve and delicacy he imparts or tries to impart to his own writing? It does not seem probable that he will, and this fact is especially applicable to translation of poetry. Writers like Akhmatova and Pasternak have shown a hesitancy towards translations when they undertook verse rendering from English into Russian, and this mood appears to prevail generally. Akhmatova went so far as to say that translation was more or less "fatal" to true creativity, and compared it to "eating your own brain." A debatable point indeed, with which those concerned may or may not agree.

Yet translation can become more effective, if greater care and thought are given to the making of the work in the recipient language. Because (to me) translations of poetry seem to offer a greater challenge and simultaneously render a sort of purer fulfilment, I should like to devote my attention in this article exclusively to the translation of poetry, and not of prose. Regardless of whether (i) the translation of poetry is worth undertaking at all, or (ii) the artistic content of the original poem stands out like the moon in a still pool, one should still be able to derive a certain satisfaction from this difficult but sensitive work. Perhaps a well-meaning recognition of the role of the translator from men of letters will help, and to this the added fruits of good payment will make the process both lucrative and dignified. I am certain that translators in Western countries are paid plentifully for their translations, something that is still unheard of in our country. Isn't it time that the translator in India stops undertaking translations altogether unless he or she is paid adequately, if not handsomely, for his or her labours?

As my experience as a translator has been in the field of Oriya poetry (into English and vice versa), I feel that a comment of mine would not be out of place, about something irksome that has been plaguing me through the years—noticeable even among those fellow contemporaries of mine I have chosen to translate. Therefore, it will not be wrong to make this positive statement: these Oriya writers whose works I have translated into English feel that the act of translation is merely an auxiliary activity of mine, something that, to all accounts, a failed poet or any other literate person may satisfactorily perform. One is apt to ask: is it possible that any person well versed in the recipient language (which is English in this case) will be able to carry out a literary metamorphosis to perfection? Isn't it more reasonable to conclude that a translator with added poetic abilities and an already strong linguistic base possesses the necessary power to carry off a literary triumph?

Nobody can deny that the poem operates on two basic levels: on the level of ideas and the level of language. The poem is an integrated expression of these two, and who can serve a poet best in translation but another poet who is able to recreate not only the words but also the emotion held inside those very words? And these two codes have to be effectively interpreted by the translator-poet, from the naked substance of experience that the original poem imposes on the translator's mind. *The act of translation, therefore, constitutes the art of balance,* and this balance is achieved precariously as the poet tries to fit his own sensibilities into the circumference of another imagination. This brings into the translation process a very subjective demand, which taxes the faculties of the translator. Nevertheless, it cannot be denied that only a poet is capable of reproducing the complex essence of poetry in another framework of thought.

It is generally believed that a verse translation is itself poetry, but whether it really is poetry or not is a questionable matter. Any poem will not move fluently into translation: my own experience reveals the many hazards and difficulties encountered in the process. My main concern being the process of conveying poetry from Oriya into English, I shall discuss some of these. For example, it is almost impossible to translate poets like Upendra Bhanja or Gangadhar Meher. In Oriya literature, the problem is of language basically—and this fact is especially noticeable with these earlier poets, poets who used language with such powers of magic and devotion that resulted in instilling in the readers' minds a divine and perhaps mystic presence. Neither Upendra Bhanja nor Gangadhar Meher used free verse, and their poems literally sag with the weight of ornamentation and alliterative sounds. Lyrical poetry such as they wrote was full of words having too many referential allusions, and was more or less ritualistic, with an incantatory tone. For that matter, I would feel uncomfortable when I heard such a poem being recited aloud, as though I were undergoing a mystic sort of experience. Even the later poets of the Oriya language, poets like Radhanath Roy, resorted to strict, musical verse forms—something that fed the poetry with a feeling of mysteriousness. Oriya diction is slow and formal, the sounds of words seem to dig into the mind and meander in the deeper layers of the imagination. Let us consider the first four lines of the poem "Chilika" by Radhanath Ray:

Utkala-kamala bilasa-dirghika
Marala malini nilambu chilika
Utkalara tuhi charu alankara
Utkala bhubane shobhara bhandara

How very clever, how concise is the construction of this verse form! And with what perfection has the poet woven the sounds of each line! How very much does each line convey, with its sensual archaic flavour! Into the four words of each line is compressed the deep passion of the poet; and how does one translate a compact verse form of this type into a foreign medium such as English? To me, a good translation into English seems almost impossible to make. For the verse resembles a many-petalled flower, each petal having its own word-significance, its individual auditory echoes. To render gems like these into English would be a futile exercise, which would only harm the poetry in the original Oriya, like an act of desecration one cannot pardon.

Similar obstacles turn into a living wall when one goes to the love lyrics that have been so popular in Oriya through the years, mainly in the form of songs (the lyrics of poets like Gopalakrishna, Banamali, Baladeba and others). Just as the sombreness of the Oriya words is an impediment to English translation in the poetry of Upendra Bhanja and his contemporaries, the sensual yet esoteric content of these love lyrics in the Oriya sound trite and insipid in a foreign context. The separation of Radha from Krishna, the forlorn waiting of Radha, and Radha's longing for union, lose their special poignancy when rendered into English. How does one explain an emotional quality inherent in *leela,* or *abhimana* or *rasa!* Here arises the fundamental difference between two distinctly separate cultures, for which no solution is apparent. And yet, translations from one regional language into another in India pose no special problems.

Coming once again to the words of a poet like Upendra Bhanja, one realises that the emphasis is on the *music* of words achieved through a verbal structure full of alliterations, assonance, and of a repetition of the sounds of words even in single lines. Here, sadly, one searches for an equivalent rhetoric and fails. The charm, the eloquence of the music in Bhanja's verse, the Oriental grace of the verse, eludes the English language. How can one portray to a Western reader the vertebrae of a culture he probably has learnt to shun through the decades? For instance, the interior of a village house, like the inside of a shell with its cramped space; the physical belongings of a rural family such as a sackful of paddy, dried-up cowdung for fuel, some dry gourd seeds—all this adds up to a picture of acceptance and contentment which is difficult to convey to a Western reader. Hedge plants like *baigaba,* medicinal plants like *basanga* or *bisalyakarani,* flowers like *gangasiuli*—these have their own referential values to the Oriya people and have been linked to ritual and worship for ages. As such, any translation which uses these words will lose their significance of deep-rooted associations; articulation is therefore incomplete in the translated versions. The numerous rituals and myths that are in common day-to-day use in Orissa are extremely hard to get across in English, and hold no relevance to the Western reader. In addition, swear-words and sayings in Oriya, many of them age-old, make the translation act harder still; one will have to leave them aside and perhaps locate approximate substitutes.

Translation of *ancient* Oriya poetry (or songs) into English becomes a heart-rending affair; understandably, therefore, the translations I have done are from the post-independence period. Free verse forms are probably easily tackled, but even a prose translation of a poem needs as much care and thought as the translation of a rhymed poem. Often, I have had to abandon metre and rhyme in translation; this perhaps only mutilates the verse, making it an unfaithful image of the original, with loss of growth of the poem and its clarity. But (and this I have found from my own experience) the quality of a translation improves with succeeding efforts; the act of translation therefore seems to be an unending one, and tends to approach the ideal after number of painstaking versions.

As I come to the end of this brief discussion, I wonder how satisfying it would be if the original poet's voice flashed in the cloudy skies of the recipient language like a searing shaft of lightning, both to the poet and to the translator. Keeping in mind that the translator has the sort of sensitivity that is needed of him to translate, he is also guided by his inner (perhaps unexplained) motive for taking up a particular translation. There must be reasons for doing so. Maybe a particular poem has something in it which excites me, creating very similar feelings and responses, and hence impels me to take up that work; or, contrarily, a totally different sort of poem defies that part of my consciousness which has lain dormant, provoking me to translate that poem. For it would not be wrong to say that the translation act is an impulsive one, depending upon the temperament of the translator. If I have, for example, chosen to translate the poetry of Sitakant Mahapatra, Soubhagya Kumar Misra and Devdas Chhotray, doesn't it smack of a selective behaviour? Why not other, equally significant, poets of the Oriya language?

But perhaps translation, with its trends for preference, holds much fulfilment—despite the difficulties, the rigours and the indifferent attitude of many of the translated poets. I should say that I have liked doing this sort of work, believing that my translations have tended towards general enjoyment rather than the completion of stuffy, scholarly versions of the original poems.

17

A Symphony in Stone

To my mind, one of the most fascinating examples of temple architecture is to be found in the tiny village of Hirapur in coastal Orissa. Its design, its imaginative oneness, and the impeccably executed sculptures set into its circular walls, make it one of the most aesthetic specimens of Orissan art. And yet the temple differs from all other Orissan temples, holding the eye of the visitor to its silent icon-centre, as he stands, mute, to its aura of revolving space without end.

But should one call it a temple in the usual sense one knows a temple? I do not know. Should I be accused of a simpering sentimentality when I speak of it? I do not know. But I am filled with an exceptional admiration for this display by Orissan temple builders and wonder at the skill, the craft of a culture which is perhaps no longer there. This is what pains one. The lost; but a presence of something passionately interesting holding these ancient stones—something for people to be queuing up outside and marvel at and which they don't.

Ringed as though by a halo of divine light, the temple dedicated to the worship of the *devi* lies amid spreading rice fields. And as one watches, something larger than life itself, something larger than God perhaps, appears to glide out of these exquisite miniatures to soften the mind in the silence of the Orissan countryside.

It is fairly easy to come to Hirapur. Close to the capital city of Bhubaneswar, one takes a mere forty minutes to drive to the village, where the temple of 64 *yoginis* is located at its far end.

The drive takes one past the old ruins of Sisupalgarh, where excavation work is still in progress near the River Daya. Past the Uttara crossroads, and then one finds oneself in the heart of rural Orissa, going down the bridge of the River Bhargavi. One is now in the village of Balakati, well known for items of brass which have been made here for years by generations of bell-metal workers. We go through the picturesque village and find ourselves on a narrow, rugged road by an irrigation canal. Wide paddy fields stretch away toward a skyline closed by rows of coconut palms. Pheasant calls sound from distant trees, interspersed with the pleasant crooning of bulbuls.

We traverse the uneven road and move slowly into the drowsy village of Hirapur, right down among the paddies. The little lane barely lets us pass, the clay houses and their straw thatches narrowing the lane further. A tranquil sight: children frolicking everywhere, monkeys chattering in the deep shade of branches and family elders watching us unconcerned from their dung-washed verandahs. Vines crowd the thatched roofs, fruiting with gourds. The drab surfaces of the walls are embellished with fanciful designs done with the white powder of ground rice; once again a ritual, a way of living for simple village women pursuing their unchanging traditions.

The constricted village path opens up suddenly into a shady grove beside a large pool, where the *Chausathi Jogini Mandira* stands, barely noticeable among the trees.

Ancient, open to the skies without its usual roof or crown, the temple is dedicated to the worship of the eternal female deity. The construction is in the form of a circle almost 30 feet in diameter. The circular stone wall is adorned on the outside with stone sculptures, evenly spaced.

But it is the inside of this edifice which strikes the visitor's eye at once. A small altar-like central structure of stone sits at the centre of this circle, exquisitely carved figures set into its corners. And all along the inner wall in rectangular niches in the stone, rest 60 of these magnificent images representing the different aspects of the *devi*. Each piece of sculpture appears to be a masterpiece of Orissan art, shaped out of sombre, dark chlorite. The images are just a half-metre high; and even though they have been exposed to the elements for over ten centuries, still retain their polish and their eloquence.

Although we do come across temples dedicated to *yogini* worship in India, only four are of significance. Besides this one at Hirapur, Orissa has another in ruins, at Ranipur-Jharial. The other two centres of *yogini* worship are at Khajuraho and Bheraghat in Madhya Pradesh. Hirapur was the first centre to have such a temple which was built in the ninth century, while the others came up later, ending with the one at Bheraghat in the tenth-eleventh centuries.

Much evidence exists today to justify that Orissa was the first seat of *tantrism* in India. Beginning from the seventh century A.D., *shakti* worship found widespread acceptance throughout the land. Manifestations of the Mother, or the *devi*, came to be known in different forms: among them Uma, Gouri, Kali, Bhavani, Rudrani, Sarbani, Sarvamangala, Aparna, Parvati, Durga, Chandika and Ambika are probably more well known.

In reality, although the number of *yoginis* is innumerable, *tantriks* appear to worship mainly the 64 manifestations of the *devi.* In these 64 are embodied the 64 arts, making the *yogini* an embodiment of yoga in the form of the woman.

It is indeed difficult to identify the 60 *yoginis* which line the inner wall of the Hirapur Temple. Careful comparison with the *Devi Purana* has only yielded partial results. As many as 26 of these images of the *devi* defy identification even today. For the ordinary visitor, however, this does not lessen the enjoyment of the aesthetics of the place. There comes a certain fulfilment in simply looking at these marvellous pieces of art, which the *Chausathi Jogini Mandira* reveals even after many centuries.

For art is substance. Love, lust, illusion. Substance in the surge of passion.

Who knows what ritual practices were performed in the dim recesses of this temple, under the wide-awake stares of these *yoginis,* beneath the midnight stars, twelve hundred years ago?

One can merely imagine the monstrous, the terrible and above everything else, the magic of it all.

The sheer geometry of the arrangement and the graceful, symbolic images of the *yoginis* haunt one long after one has left the village. I marvel at the proportions of the execution, as though each one of the 60 odd sculptures had attained the ideal even in the presence of the grotesque which helps to establish the nature of the deity. Perhaps, always, architectural grace was a concept known to the old temple builders of Orissa. I remember the words from the *Silpa Prakasa:*

Desire is the root of the universe. From desire all beings are born...

18

This Sadness is Mine Also

There was his face in the clean and humble darkness, a haunted blur in the starlight of an October evening, a mysterious presence in the silence of this quiet little village nestling among the trees. His head, his slender frame were covered in a coarse, cotton sheet.

It wasn't possible for me to discern his features clearly, for there was an absence of light, the light to which my eyes had been accustomed through years of town and city living. I looked up into his face: it was all earth, and the seasons seemed to hang about it, winter and summer, and the long, savage rains of the mountain ranges of eastern India.

It was only October, I thought, but the air was already cold. A fire burned a little distance away, and gathered around it was a small group of people taking in the comforting warmth from the orange coals. Incoherent babblings drifted into my ears.

The village of Paraja Limika lies among rolling stretches of fields of broken grain at the edge of the hills that are so much a distinctive part of the landscape of Koraput in Orissa. In front of it, a narrow, uneven ridge drops steeply to the path among the fields and to the slippery, cramped crossing across the rocky stream to the slightly wider path that runs for a distance of three kilometres or more to the asphalted highway near Dumuriput.

A cool wind blew in from the east. I had decided to see for myself these villages in the interior of Orissa, and we had managed to borrow a friend's scooter to cover the eight kilometres along the wide highway that runs from the newly-built township of Sunabeda to the headquarters town of Koraput.

It was an exhilarating ride to Dumuriput, for the landscape, imperturbable and composed, seems to expand, filling the mind. The fresh, clean mountain air does wonders for tired, frayed nerves.

This region of the Kolab is peacefully picturesque: one hill slope leads unobtrusively to another, the green meadow grass rising and falling in swells. And the hills here are uncommon; they are perfectly rounded, elemental, rising up from the surrounding plain, shaped like women's breasts—dusky and bashful, like the faces of tribal girls one encounters often in these parts.

The waters of a newly-built dam on the upper reaches are slowly spreading across the countryside, flooding fields and villages—a tranquil scene to a town visitor, but a scene in which lay hidden the grief-wracked lives of hundreds of villagers uprooted from their age-old ancestral holdings.

We parked our scooter at Dumuriput and walked the five-plus kilometres along the uneven ridge winding through the fields of grain and flowers. The sun was on the point of going down behind the hills and our draggy walk had led us to the bank of a muddy stream. The ecstatic shouts of girls frolicking in the water in front of us reverberated through the sparse, silent air. They were girl *coolies* coming back home from their daily work at the site of a railway line that was being laid; unconcerned about our stares, they went on washing themselves in the stream.

We stood there for a while, curious, amazed, watching the reckless abandon of the girls as they swam up and down a 50-metre stretch of the stream. The present was all theirs: the moments in the water were theirs, and those moments were true.

I waited on the bank for a few minutes, thinking of a way to go across. There was no other way but to wade through the water at the shallower sections of the river. Gingerly, we removed our shoes, rolled our trouser cuffs as far up as we could and stepped into the water.

The water was muddy with the girls' movements. Bemused, they looked on as I took my first unsure steps, groping with my feet. Suddenly, a young girl shouted, "Not there, *babu!* Go a little ahead... Yes, there!" And she burst into peals of laughter.

We went across the stream, carrying our shoes in our hands. Meanwhile, the girls had finished their baths and were already walking ahead of us, their brisk strides in unison with their lithe young bodies.

There were still a couple of kilometres to cover before we reached the village. A dim light lay over the entire landscape. On either side stretched undulating patches of earth; the *mandia* (a type of easy-growing grain favoured by the tribals) was beginning to bud, and the irresistibly lovely golden *alasi* was already in flower.

The girls now had an almost 50-metre lead. Their walk seemed to cut through the darkening, huddled stillness; and their songs, strange, shrouded and shrill, played among the clustered crowns of the *alasi.* The songs, I soon realised, were impromptu, made up then and there; the words were simple, and in them was buried the spirit of a simple person, the spirit of earth and wind and fire:

> From somewhere these babus come
> Who are they who can tell?
> Where they go, perhaps we know,
> These babus with shoes in their hands.

A sadness fills me as I watch the trembling blooms of *alasi,* as I watch the mud-coloured backs of the departing girls, and I can't understand why. It amazes me that I am much past the prime of my life. I stand outside the sweeping quiet and sense the autumn evening go away with them into the wreaths of darkness.

Paraja Limika was one of the first villages I had chosen to visit on my recent wanderings around Koraput and Kalahandi. Geographically, it is quite close to the spacious Sunabeda township, about 12 kilometres away. I wanted to see for myself how time had affected the dreams of a simple folk who slept under the feeling of vastness and endless days, how a newly-ushered-in technology had changed their lives in recent years.

The face in the darkness looked down at me where I was seated, on a flat, circular slab that served as the centre of all activities of the village. Slowly, as we had waited, several people had gathered around; a mysterious deadness appeared to lie on their faces, so quietly had they crept in during the few minutes we had been there.

His name was Bala Jani, the face answered in reply to my question. The evening's stars seemed to regard us with silent amusement. A sudden screeching of owlets in the nearby trees sounded like curses in the tattered dark.

"How old are you?" I asked. "Seventy something, I think," he answered.

The others mumbled in agreement. The huts stood around us, like unnatural growths from the rocky ground, and a wood fire was visible through the blurred depths. Some concern was apparent in Bala Jani's voice, for he asked,

"Why have you come all the way in the dark? What can you see now in the night? And what is there to see here?"

He wrapped his cloak closely about him and appeared to grimace at us. Maybe the villagers didn't want intruders at all, town visitors as we were. Did I detect a smile of scorn of his features?

I don't know if he believed my words, that my interest in them was sincere. It would be wrong to blame him if he thought me to be a liar. I must have seemed an exploiter of some sort, like one of those who came to canvass for votes at election time.

"The old days were better," Bala Jani asserted. "Nothing has happened to us through the years for us to tell you." My prodding about the independence of the country and the changes this had brought about seemed meaningless then, perhaps obscene. Bala Jani looked away.

His impatient gaze shows through the wasted flesh of his ancient body. Spent things, leftovers. I could sense strange flickerings in the cave of his mind.

Perhaps nothing had happened to Paraja Limika in these years. The village lay a mere five kilometres away from the new, concrete toll gate on the highway; still it remained as it had always been, infected with darkness. There was still no road to link the village with either Koraput or Sunabeda. You had to cross the sullen river, and take the foot-wide ridge that wound up and down across the fields to reach the village. The river was a constant hazard; only the year before, an elder called Badi Mali had tried to cross it but was swept away and had drowned.

"Couldn't you see that a bridge is built across this stream?" Bala Jani ventured to ask. I had no answer. It would be fairly easy to build one across this 30-feet wide river, I told myself, but none had been built so far. The others who had crowded around went on to say that all the water for their daily needs came from the same stream.

"The nearest tubewell is 12 kilometres away," Bala Jani added quietly.

I stared at him, wondering at the absurdity of it all. The interiors of Koraput and Kalahandi were by and large inaccessible, with dense jungles and hilly terrain, and there were innumerable villages scattered all over, some of them impossible to reach during the rains. Paraja Limika was situated on the edge of the well laid-out town of Sunabeda—a place where sophisticated aero-engines were manufactured. If these were the conditions in Paraja Limika, I thought, one could imagine just what was happening in the remote regions of Orissa.

"All right," I put in after a while. "But what about the children in the village? Don't you send them to school?"

We had observed a dilapidated mud hut on our way to the village, somewhere on the outskirts, and had wondered what it was. It became clear to us now that it was the village primary school.

"There is a school, there, beyond," Bala Jani said, unnecessarily pointing with his hand into the dark. "But the teacher seldom comes. And when he does, once in a week almost, it's around noon and the children are rarely there. Can we blame our children if they are not present when the teacher comes?"

Our proddings revealed that the school was established about twelve years ago, but the school-teacher rarely came to coach the students. There had been no visits of the school inspector; and if any inspections had taken place, nobody knew anything about it. It was pathetic indeed.

When I went back to Sunabeda and resumed my inquiries about the school later on, I found out that the school teacher had a profitable little business on the side in the town. Nevertheless, he received his teacher's salary without fail at the beginning of every month. He made a fairly comfortable living and no guilt of any sort appeared to touch him.

Is this life, then, for a simple person in a village situated close to a prosperous industrial township—a life so anonymous and sloppy, lacking respect and awareness? Does such a life make sense, does it stand to reason in 1987?

I felt the torment rising in me, felt it answered in the hooded eyes of Bala Jani and the other villagers. I looked at the torn, grave face of the old *mukhia* of Paraja Limika and thought: this sadness is mine also, one I did not realise before, one I do not know how to counter today.

Paraja Limika, and its magic in the eyes of women when the silver dance of the autumn moonlight was upon them. I will always remember this, and the veil of peace, the sensual abandon of its world. Yet, all this could not overcome the poverty of the village, among the rocky fields of *mandia* which the people make into a gruel for their daily needs.

Nothing, I told myself, has changed here in these 40 years; the huts are dark, there is no light, no water, and nothing for the future of the famished, mud-hued children hanging from the dark trees. Only the old women and men, with their hands like gnarled roots reaching forward toward their young, as their minds drift uncertainly into waking dreams of feasting in luxurious city banqueting halls.

Night had fallen without our realising it. A villager led us across the bouncy path along the fields for a while until we gratefully bade him goodbye. We were under the earth's own stars, and the stream we had crossed earlier bared itself in the faint starlight. I remembered my own self, losing myself in memories of past and present, knowing I would live on as I had always lived writing the poems that meant nothing at all—poems which a few close friends of mine might read some day and realise were not only useless but pointless.

Corruption is not in the way people everywhere make their thousands and lakhs, I concluded. It is in the way each one of us makes use of the situation we are in. And, in our country, we are already experiencing the worst form of corruption—not the monetary form with which we are all familiar, but the corruption inherent in the fact that the wrong persons are in places—in the state and in society—which demanded the appropriate decision and actions for such people, and which always worked to the detriment of our people as a whole.

One, like me, ultimately tries to escape facing such a state of affairs. As I walked back, I kept thinking how there had been no progress after the country's independence in villages like Paraja Limika.

The sky seemed to lower above me. In the distance, an orangish glow lighted up the horizon. It would be Sunabeda, I thought. A thousand doubts gnawed inside me. My mind appeared drained, unable to take in the clear harmony of earth and sky. There were just the dismal shapes of mountains around us, rising even over the clouds, like politicians or bureaucrats—enslavers of a greater land in the darkness of India.

19

A Book from My Shelf

It is in the mind that the true enjoyment of a book lies. The mind, so much an unknown thing itself, about whose workings we do not know, but can hold so much. The mind, which can expand to unimaginable limits, bringing in joy or sorrow, pain and grief, or a peace beyond description; inspired by that adventure held between the covers of a book. And beyond all, our dreams, which the mind can arouse.

It should not be difficult for anyone to see why I have chosen this particular book from my shelves to talk about today. We still live in distressed times. The countryside in India appears to be polluted not merely by the incursions of industry and technology. However, when we give this some serious thought, it becomes apparent that the pollution comes from inside, through hunger and starvation.

So I have picked up Kamala Markandaya's novel, *Nectar in a Sieve,* an ageing paperback I possess, and which I had bought way back in 1956. Its pages are discoloured through the years, but the book retains its uniqueness in poetic beauty, in its restrained and controlled tragedy. In effect, it is a touching novel, that holds within its pages the truth of pure, clean experience. And it really feels good that I should be talking about it almost fifty years after its first publication.

Perhaps hunger is the main theme in *Nectar in a Sieve.* In this respect the book can be easily placed alongwith some other highly rated novels, such as Bhabani Bhattacharya's *So Many Hungers* for its portrayals of the degradation of humanity; with the Nobel Prize winning writer Pearl Buck's *The Good Earth* for the treatment of milieu and environment; and with Prem Chand's *Godaan* for its sincere, realistic approach. This beautiful and eloquent story tells of a simple peasant woman in a primitive village in India whose entire life was a gallant and persistent battle to care for those she loved.

Married as a child-bride to a tenant farmer she had never seen, she worked side by side in the field with her husband to wrest a living from land that was ravaged by droughts, monsoons, and insects. With remarkable fortitude and courage, she sought to meet changing times and fight poverty and disaster. She saw one of her infants die from starvation, her daughter become a prostitute, and her sons leave the land for jobs which she never trusted.

Even through the realistic approach Kamala Markandaya adopted for her novel, the many themes she has treated therein reflect the plight of the ideal as well as the actual world conceived by her. Hunger and poverty are the two main axes between which rural problems like food, drought, superstition, social inequality, illiteracy, exploitation and the struggle for survival build up. And how impeccably does the South Indian village of Markandaya symbolise any rural place existing on Indian soil, even today? What is remarkable is the balance Kamala Markandaya has been able to achieve with these elements; for a reader like me, in this lies the genuine power of her rural realism.

Yet what stands out throughout her work is the undeniable, sheer magic of her words. I cannot but quote some passages from the book—the purity and gentle movement of the language wrings the heart. The very beginning of the novel is a slow flow of feeling. A special poignancy comes through quietly. I quote:

> Sometimes at night I think that my husband is with me again, coming gently through the mists, and we are tranquil together. Then morning comes, the wavering grey turns to gold, there is a stirring within me as the sleepers awake, and he softly departs.

Nectar in a Sieve is one long narrative of Rukmani, the peasant woman, who never loses her faith in life or her love for her husband and children—despite her endless battle against relentless nature, changing times, and dire poverty. Rukmani doesn't quite know how to face her life. "But how?" she muses. "We have no money. My husband can till and sow and reap with skill, but here there is no land. I can weave and spin, or plait matting, but there is no money for spindle, cotton, or fibre. For where shall a man turn who has no money? Where can he go? Wide, wide world, but as narrow as the coins in your hand. Like a tethered goat, so far and no farther. Only money can make the rope stretch, only money."

I am reminded of our own rural villages in Orissa that have been ravaged by rain and floods, by droughts and famine. Kamala Markandaya's village could easily be mine, or yours. And in this thought lies the everlasting quality of her book.

For hunger observes no rules of humanity or quality. I'd like to quote again:

> For hunger is a curious thing: at first it is with you all the time, waking and sleeping and in your dreams, and your belly cries out insistently, and there is a gnawing and a pain as if your very vitals were being devoured, and you must stop it at any cost, and you buy a moment's respite even while you know and fear the sequel. Then the pain is no longer sharp but dull, and this too is with you always... Then that too is gone, all pain, all desire, only a great emptiness is left, like the sky, like a well in drought...

Maybe very personal reasons bind me to Markandaya's novel. I remember my grandfather, as a sixteen-year-old, starving and on the point of death, struggling for any edible plant or root he could find, during the fearful famine that swept through Orissa in 1866. It is almost impossible for me to forget my own personal history. The delineation of the motif of hunger explicitly remains one of the pre-eminent features of *Nectar in a Sieve.* This theme has been dealt with more sympathetically, more realistically than many other post-independence novels where the struggle is between man and the sufferings from starvation.

There is a humbling power in Markandaya's book that I experienced. And yet *Nectar in a Sieve* does not end in a note of despair. There is a touch of benediction I found, a form of blessing which conquered me. I end with this quote from her book:

> In that field, in the grain which had not yet begun to form,
> lay our future and our hope.

20

Letter from Orissa to *The Hudson Review* (New York), 1987

March in India signifies a time for beginnings, a time when the koel's haunting cry reverberates through the clear skies, and the trees, full of new leaf, tremble as mysterious sobs enter their throats from the depths of the earth. At this time too, the old year according to the Indian calendar comes to an end. Joyous festivals mark the new year, as side by side with sweeping celebrations, feverish transactions continue in commercial houses and government offices for the closure of another "financial" year.

Now the cricketing season is over too, and the papers and magazines are still discussing the recent defeats of the Indian team by Pakistan, both here at home and in the Middle East. Analyses by sports commentators fill the back pages, pictures of cricket "stars" stare out from the glossies in the bookstands, even their faces are used for publicity purposes by the government-controlled television. In quiet contrast to all this, and against the mad killings which go on almost every day in the northwestern state of Punjab, a peaceful little festival was being held in the central region of the country—a festival of subdued poetry readings and deliberations that brought out into the open the Indian poet's responsibility to the society he lives in, and where poets from all over India meditated on justice, love and humanity.

The occasion was *Kavibharati,* the first ever Triennale of Indian poetry. Here, from 28 to 30 March, in near-idyllic surroundings, as the cool evening breezes of March floated in across the large tranquil lake and the lights jewelled the minarets on the far shores, something else came into life besides the sound of the modest wash of waters against the rocks. It was a quiet statement for the restoration of our faith in the creative arts. For three days sensitive poetic activity perhaps made us think of those things we had wanted sometime to say; three days in which the magic of the mind fluttered like a pennant in the pain-soaked sky of Bhopal. And one felt the sadness still, as one heard the words of fifty poets who had gathered for the occasion, and the sadness seemed to settle over the gleaming new complex of the Centre for the Arts at Bharat Bhavan.

So *Kavibharati* began, and ended, without much publicity. We heard and waited, we stood back and we saw, in the words of the Urdu poet Shamsur Rahman Faruqi: "Night buys us for peanuts. / Night falls with a broken wing."

What *did* eventually emerge, I ask myself, from the many sessions of readings and the seminars on the role of poetry? Nothing really perhaps, and yet, at the end a simmering dissatisfaction at the way literatures in the various languages of the country were taking us.

I suppose it would not be wrong to suggest that poetry in the regional languages began changing only after the *new poem*, with its emotional but strongly intellectual content, found its way into the country. Modernism, where abstraction and concreteness could be successfully interlinked, swayed the heads of these English-educated writers—their gods were Eliot and Yeats. On the west coast of India, writing in Marathi, Vinda Karandikar spoke of "The Traitor":

> He gulps down his daily ration of liquid fire
> Served by the morning papers,
> And then to expiate the sin
> Fingers the love-locks of children;
> Reads the *Gita* and warns himself

"Don't you touch a weapon. Beware!"
Opens his umbrella to remember
Only the nuclear mushroom,
Places his hand on somebody's shoulder
Just to regain his balance.

From Kerala, on the southwestern tip of the peninsula, the voice belonged to K. Satchidanandan, who grouched in his native Malayalam:

But he who has been out in the world
Finds no peace at home.
I am a tombstone now, spiritless, dead.

And the distinguished Kannada poet, Gopala Krishna Adiga, asked in his poem "The Earth Is Not Flat":

All the waters of pool, river
Well or gutter become one.
Tell me where do you find castes?
Isn't it when you are rooted in the soil?

More than two decades ago, when Ronald Segal went on to discuss and reinterpret attitudes toward India in his book, *The Anguish of India,* readers seemed doubtful about what they read; for no longer did India stand forth as a beacon of truth. Instead, the same dark forces of superstition and irrationality appeared to obstruct the attainment of an ordered society. Segal put forward his concern competently when he asked: "Will India have an Indian government ruthless enough to rule in the interests of the still silent masses?" Today, as we near the end of the eighties, the same anguish and indignation that plagued Segal's social conscience eat into the heart of every sensitive individual concerned with finding a solution for the country's persistent ills. The strong government which Segal hoped for has not come into existence even forty years after India gained her independence. It is indeed tragic that we have not been able to produce such a government, one which would help to control all significant aspects of human life. The indifference to human suffering is evident everywhere, even today, and it becomes difficult to close one's eyes to this continuing trait of the Indian upper classes—this "final denial of humanity" which Segal exposed so honestly in his book.

Caste, colour consciousness and a fanatical puritanism are aspects of our living that drag us down to the depths of our being even today. If we consider further the dimensions of hunger and sexuality which still plague our lives, it is easy to understand why, despite honorable exceptions, so much contemporary writing in India appears old-fashioned and unexciting. It would not be wrong to state that most Indian poetry and fiction continue to be inhibited by an inexplicable romanticism. Is this, I wonder, mainly because of the Indian sensibility, because of an intrinsic desire to put together and experience the Primal Unity, because of a persistent feeling of sanctity and sacredness that mark *karuna* and *ahimsa*? Generally speaking, the Indian mind still takes refuge in the cloudy symbols of fatalism; the average reader or listener is unlikely to be swayed by bare, brutal poetry.

As I come to the end of this letter I realise how incomplete and haphazard it has been. India is too vast a country, too fragmented in some ways, for one region to know much about another. Very little material is available in translation. The past few years have witnessed the publication of some books in English translation, but this work too is disoriented.

As a writer who uses English, I have often been asked: "Why do you write in English in India?" This simple question opens up large areas of debate. Perhaps we'll leave that for another time. But it would only be right to mention that in India more books are published in English than in any other language.

And here is a question I'd like answered. Is there any other country in the world whose President or Prime Minister releases a book every other day, throughout the year?

21

Of the Lowly Potato: Indian English Poetry Today

If you can get down to its essence, even a lowly potato would be poetic.

What is remarkable is that poetry can prove it.

In India, in the post-independence era, innumerable collections of poetry written in English have appeared from various publishing houses. Certainly more than the volumes of prose that have been published so far. The point is: It is an odd situation, because more bad poetry is being published now than ever before in Indian history. And whereas our fiction has made a decisive impact on literary writing around the world, nothing very significant has been seen in the output of Indian poetry written in English.

The reasons for this would appear to lie in the writing of poetry itself. One sees the evidence of poetry's diminished stature even within the practice of poetry. There are very few magazines in our country that publish poetry today. And even in the ones that do, one's heart sinks to see so many poems crammed so tightly together, like sardines packed in a small can. It would be easy to miss a radiant poem among the many mediocre ones. It takes much effort to read these little magazines with openness and attention. Few people bother, not even the magazine's contributors. The sheer indifference to poetry in the mass media has created a sort of Frankenstein—magazines that publish poetry unwisely, with total indiscretion.

The other characteristic that catches the eye is the overwhelmingly *positive* prose that is being written about published collections of poetry. These reviews or comments and essays *do not* (I stress, *do not*) provide an objective perspective on new poetry volumes, which is what is required, but simply publicise them. Quite often there are manifest personal connections between the reviewers (or editors) and the authors they discuss. The unspoken editorial rule seems to be: Do not give negative views; they are, after all, our friends and colleagues, and we cannot afford to hurt them.

The consequence of all this seriously affects the thinking and make-up of the beginner-poet in our country. These emerging poets (and we are full of such writers and readers) are seemingly confused by seeing mediocre poetry praised, or never criticised—and in the long run end up doubting their own critical perceptions. Younger poets, therefore, start emulating the work of these poets, writing in the same manner. This is a dangerous process that has only resulted in betraying the integrity of the art of writing poetry. Very recently I came across an editorial comment in one of our larger circulated weeklies, which stated that a particular collection of poems "was easily the best volume of poems published by an Indian in recent years." This is a strong statement indeed, but made in a casual vein. Statements such as these should be substantiated. Books are read, and ultimately, judged by individuals in the privacy of their own sensibilities, and not by committees who talk about cricket and Kargil and poetry in the same vein. Evaluation is always hard, serious work. And by going about it frivolously, we only demean our own art.

But why should anyone but a poet care about the problems of Indian poetry? What relevance does this archaic art form have to contemporary society? If ours would have been a more tolerant, better world than what it is today, then poetry would have no need to justify itself beyond the sheer splendour of its existence. Does our world vindicate the American poet Wallace Stevens's words that "the purpose of poetry is to contribute to man's happiness?" But perhaps aesthetic pleasure needs no justification, because a life without such pleasure is one not worth living.

Poets are expected to make sense of life. If they find life today in fragments, they must not leave it that way. Perhaps they should have that desire to produce poetry that transcends the ills of modern life rather than poetry that helplessly mirrors them. It is easy for me to say this when I know I am guilty myself of such writing. But I am afraid this is a difficult task to achieve.

Indian poetry in English lacks ideas. Again, I realise this is a foolish statement which leaves much room for error. Let us all agree that our poems are characterised by a thinness. Somehow almost all our poems sound alike. And barring the poems of a few, these poems exhibit a one-dimensionality that reveals their meanings straightaway. Missing are the many levels of meaning that give strength and intensity to a poem. Do our poets ever attempt, in Hardy's phrase, "to touch our hearts by revealing their own"? Maybe they don't do that.

Sadly, Indian poetry in English does not touch us in our deepest, most enduring self.

I believe our poetry—by this I imply Indian poetry in English—will not be held in high esteem until we explore our writing within the context of a unifying outlook on life. It is easy to make poems that are urged by sporadic, individual responses to things—to write a poem on the potato I mentioned earlier; but perhaps to seek an insight into the potato's mind that is haunted by the sinister density of the earth. Perhaps we never try to seek that experience and perception that make up for what we call the poet's "vision". I do not know how to define these things. But this way of going into the meaning of the insight is more likely to be achieved slowly and naturally as a result *of simply living and responding to things in the world,* of reading and thinking, and in the daily work of writing poems.

Every poet seeks to accomplish something like this in the poems he or she writes, or else he or she would not be able to write at all. But he or she should not build his or her life by finding himself or herself in another country, in another history, or elsewhere. Simply speaking, one's own roots are of the utmost importance although one's work is in English. One of the strengths of poetry in Spanish in our time is that it has not lost contact with the past. Quevedo and Gongora are still living presences for poets in Spain and South America, as they were for Lorca and others of his generation.

It wouldn't be wrong to say that there is a distinct absence of vitality in our poetry. All our competence with words and with craft, with images and metaphors, asks for *substance;* and purpose beyond mere versification is what is called for. Our poetry must be involved with us, with the many lives we live. Perhaps our prose just possesses that; it makes us participate in the myth-processes of our people—and this aspect accounts for its success in the present day.

If we accept the fact that English poetry in India has taken a definite direction today, we could trace its influence to a few poets who were teachers of English literature themselves. Nissim Ezekiel could be considered to lead this poetry movement; he was followed by A.K. Ramanujan, R. Parthasarathy and Shiv K. Kumar, if I would name some. Today, we have a number of younger poets who seem to be influenced by the terse craftwork exhibited by their elders. If we examine these poems, we find an excessive use of wit and irony in them. It is difficult not to notice the distance this poetry reveals, as compared to the poems of poets in the many regional languages of India. Also is evident a lack of musicality in the poems. Somehow I believe that music is the most important virtue in poetry, and this appears to be absent. I will not go into the reasons behind this. But it seems right I should speak about my own experiences in this regard.

In the fiftieth year of our independence, the British magazine titled *London Magazine* appeared with a special issue with the words *INDIA 1997: with affection* on its cover. This magazine is now in its 39th year and is edited by Alan Ross. A look into this issue gives us an insight into the type of poetry the editor likes to publish. I am afraid I have to admit that the poetry here conforms to the qualities I mentioned earlier. I should like to confess that my poetry didn't find a place in this issue. The fact is: I didn't send my poems for this issue. And if I had sent my work, I am certain the editor would have rejected my poems, as he had done twice before, twenty years back. The ironic mode has never suited me, and I have chosen to write what I wrote, straight from my heart. Maybe this isn't good, well-crafted poetry—the poetry I write. I could never respond to the sight of Nandi in the manner a poem "Pashupatinath" goes on to depict the scene (pp 178-179):

> A bull of beaten gold
> balanced on balls
> so large they dwarfed
>
> the nesting crowds.
> With hands full of money,
> flowers and prayers,
>
> our unruly lines
> mobbed the priest...
> ...

Or, as in the poem "One or Two Places" on page 63 of the issue:

> If you love your country, he said,
> why are you here?
> Say, I am tired of hearing about
>
> all that wonder that was India
> kind of crap...

And incidentally, I remember Alan Ross, the editor, having written me on a 5 cm by 10 cm rejection slip, when he had returned my poems, that my work was unsuitable for publication because it tended to be philosophic. My own writing has always reflected an Oriya sensibility and I have felt myself to be an Oriya poet who happened to write in English. I suppose our sensibility, the Indian sensibility, is different from the Western one, and this fact stands in the way of the Western reader. This is an area where the Indian mind turns its antennae toward the unknown, the *beyond,* making the resulting poetry lose its concreteness, and the verse becomes dependent on suggestions of meaning. This is one reason why some of my work comes back from editors of foreign journals.

However, it was in the eighties or early nineties that a change was seen in much of the English poetry written in India. The discerning reader no longer wanted to read merely a well-crafted poem of an Indian poet in English, a poem which could have come as well from the pen of a poet living in Britain or Australia. Neither was the poet interested only in the dry wit and irony most Indian-English poems exhibited. The prevailing poetry scene was witnessing a subtle change. Poets, younger poets, from various parts of the country were coming our with their poems; suddenly, English poems were being written differently in Kerala, in the northeast, and in my own state of Orissa. It was the native culture showing in the poem of the Indian English poet. It was a poetry which eased itself from the earth the poet inhabited, nurtured and nourished by the soil and the air of the place. There was a distinct sense of belonging; it couldn't be mistaken:

> On a warm day at the start of spring
> men in the fields feel winter
> melting in their blood too,
>
> they smell the seed of ripeness in the air
> and nod to each other happily,
> or take up the children, kiss their
>
> dusty heads and let them go again.
> Evening comes. Everything happens naturally
>
> as leaves closing, or the breaking of stars,
> hesitant and white, as if long ago somebody
> was hurt by their pleasure.
> ...

Or, as in this poem:

> We heard whatever is not lost.
> We speak of a mythic time.
> Let us speak of what we found:
> In the place of gold-dust we found still
> golden ears of rice beneath that copper haze
> of dying years, dancing to the valley's
>   wind-borne music;
> beacons of wild fires we saw on dry autumn nights,
> mountains signalling the fates of trees and grass.
> Instead of pages of heroic deeds or undying love,
> we read parchments written in blood, our history
> stained by illicit love and betrayal;
> we found our alphabet buried with the shrunken heads
> of enemies, ghosts who died long ago laughing
> at the attempts at civilisation.

Here, at last, the poet is speaking to me. This is poetry one likes to read, to hear. A poetry that should last.

22

A Note on Ayyappa Paniker's Poetry

It is an evening in June. The rains have just come, bringing in a cool ness to my senses. Flowers in my sleep, because I feel I'll sleep well tonight after many days. Noises of people passing by in the street across my house, the joyful shout of a child, the silence of my ninety-two-year-old mother in the next room, and the truths of poems lying on my table—poems I have read and reread and wish to write about now. These are strange crossings indeed, and movements into which I'm drawn to. It's difficult to say how we move in this world, between imagination and reality, bewildered as we are about the happenings in our society, realising well we've failed to come anywhere near our original social goals through all these years. Living with our poems, not believing our words are written on water, as we go on to seek our visions, but never quite obtaining them.

To my mind, Ayyappa Paniker has achieved considerable literary success, by any standards. For one like me who has followed his work through the years, almost across three decades, albeit in English translation, the feeling of fulfilment that comes through when one reads his poems, is uppermost. As a serious poet, he has never presented an over-optimistic view of society to his readers. Perhaps by a sort of stark, strident emphasis on the challenges he has faced, and on stressing the honesty that is behind his time and which makes him find its expression, Paniker portrays the processes of change. He is keenly aware of the experience of repeated betrayal, failures and hazards in the country in which he lives; he knows that when he is writing a poem he is involved with creating a self, a self which is under constant revision, and that he cannot lie to himself, ever.

So that is how Paniker's poetry in Malayalam impresses the reader; his forms are always varied, always changing, from a straightforward poem like "Freedom" where he uses a figurative language to mix with the formulation of that anger or "whatever" might be the driving emotion, to an intensely lyrical verse. Here is an example of the former I was speaking about, quoted in its entirety:

> The heavy gates
> of the stone prisons
> were wide open.
> Even the roofs
> had blown off.
>
> But the six o' clock siren
> was not heard.
>
> When the light of the sun
> pierced the prison chambers,
> the inmates didn't wake up.
> They waited for the siren.
>
> When the time came
> for them to queue up for lunch,
> the prisoners didn't get up.
> Not knowing they were prisoners,
> they waited for the bell.
>
> Long after the day had burnt down,
> and the double-tongued darkness
> licked away the light of the stars,
> to the inmates it was not yet daybreak.
>
> How are they to know it's dawn,
> without orders from above.

Paniker doesn't say a word more than is necessary. His wit and pith and what they imply, especially in the last two lines, is a revelation. I do not need to ask myself whether he contains the empty future of the country. But the raging power is hidden, ominous, for those who care to see.

And when one turns to the lyrical Paniker, one cannot but feel that poetry is not only a purpose with him, but a disturbing passion. There are lines I would have loved to write myself, compelling and mysterious, from the long poem for example, "Holiday Whispers: The Rahu Phase". The poem holds an area of light with all its music, and the reader forgets, alongwith the poet, whether the real world is there before him or is in a state of annihilation:

> in the end, bereft of me, alone you wait
> on the terrace of your new house for the lights of the sky,
> watching the bright glow of the moon fade away,
> seeing the night's darkness blacken the earth and sky,
> the heart breaks to think of you as a child-star
> in the midst of the dark, like a forlorn bride,
> a muffled crack is heard, and the entire universe
> startles, the eight directions tremble,
> while the earth comes to a standstill.

There is an energy here (and in the whole poem) which, undeniably, borders on the erotic. Maybe I am carried away when I read it; but how cleverly Paniker has used the elements of language to create a visual reality! It reminds me of the Greek poet, Yannis Ritsos, who in one of his poems, mixes the chronology of narrative with the pleasures of lyric and the prismatic promises of the mind:

> So, what is the good of sorrow, of hatred,
> of freedom, of the lack of freedom,
> the silver spoons, savings,
> the gold false teeth of the dead woman, the sun,
> the two candle holders on the table, aspirins,
> love, poetry?

Of course Ritsos's poem pursues his own case for a meaninglessness in life, as is apparent with the use of the words "love, poetry?" In Paniker's poem, one notices how "forlorn bride" and "the earth comes to a standstill" enlarge the poem's social context (here I am unable to quote other pertinent phrases from the rest of the poem), and how beauty contains decay ("the rainbow hope wet with moonlight sweat?"). The poem is my favorite; its images constantly surprise, juxtaposing questions of value and valuelessness. Such a poem is in direct contrast to an attitude evident in "O Mother Benign and Ferocious" where he commits himself by saying:

> Leaders, selfish and opportunistic, tell us
> That life is for doing good,
> That good is nothing but social good.
> If we are clever in spreading the net,
> We can have a good haul.

There appears to be an overt statement of purpose here, or of judgement, or emotion. Paniker's poetry is never too full of statement. The best Indian poetry—and by Indian, would refer to the poetry written in the many regional languages we have—works through mystery or suggestion, and there is enough of one or both in Paniker's oeuvre.

In an early article Ayyappa Paniker wrote on the poetry of the Indian English poet, Nissim Ezekiel, he spoke of a "third vision" which he seemed to suggest came from Ezekiel's understanding of the Psalms of David. Such an integrated vision is apparent in a reading of Paniker's poems, where he uses irony in an old fashioned way and with a content of conceit. Perhaps a plain poem like "Prison" demonstrates his sense of the sacredness of his purpose, in lines like

> the day is a prison for the night:
> the sky for the wind, the face for the eyes,
> the stomach for hunger, the mind for thoughts,
> . . .
> the picture for the eye,
> the soft scent for the nostrils,
> the hair for adorning flower,
> every word a prison for the tongue,
> your encircling arms are a prison for me.

To my mind, this is a poem which goes far beyond irony, and wit—the wit critics have extolled when speaking of Paniker's poetry. The simultaneity of experience is a feature which holds a strong attraction for the poet, as in the above poem; and it becomes easy to see how he can leave the reader inside the deeper meaning that exists beyond the seemingly simplicity of his lines. And how easily, how safely he can be, in his embrace of life on earth.

As I write this brief piece, I realise painfully I am not the right person to speak on the poetry of Ayyappa Paniker. I feel inadequate. Above all things, it is not easy to write on the work of a friend, who I have known for thirty years. I understood poetry rather late in my life. As I stand here on this monsoon evening, miles away from Kerala, I see things with my eyes and my body. This makes quite a difference in perceptions. And it is the moment that makes me see things in the way I do, realising well that I could not see them in the same way the next moment or forever. It is not easy to find yourself in a poem unless you wrote it.

But Paniker's poems have helped me to see the world through implication. Once, on another drizzling afternoon in Kottayam, he had talked to me of his childhood days and pointed out where he used to stay and move around —as we looked out from a fourth floor hotel room. The tops of coconut palms and the wet rooftops appeared alive with raindrops, dream, birdsong and church bells. Paniker was standing there at the window, going back, down his years, and had stopped time awhile. Still, in his poems there are lines:

> Going back is out of the question
> That riverside of many years ago
> will not be there any more
> ...
> it will remain empty for ever,
> the empty heart
> unblossomed, unfaded...

where the dominant mode is one of nostalgic desire. As a reader I am moved. What more can one ask for? But the poems of Paniker I will remember most clearly are those that have enacted the experience of the moment. Those flowers in my sleep. Tonight.

23

Cuttack: Smoke and a Sunset of Rivers

Cuttack, in late November, about which I wish to write. This city of mine, which they say is a thousand years old. There is nothing, they also say, that is happening in this old city in late November. The festivals have all ended; a period of timeless and unchanging rites that begins with the first monsoon rain in June until the advent of the short winter: a period of joy and light, or spending and feasting, of ecstasy and celebration. A time that holds the wondrous femininity of Cuttack, as if the city's mystical feminine half, dormant so long, had come into its own. A time starting with the festival of Durga Puja, undimmed in its spectacle through the years, where the goddess Durga is worshipped alongwith other deities. A time that brings people of all walks of life together, through ritual, through profound memory. And a time that brings a smile on faces of young and old, on the faces of naked, hungry urchins who live along the banks of the smelly, murky canal passing through the heart of this city, their eager eyes bold and undefeated.

Slowly the festival of Durga Puja slips by, unnoticed, into another quieter occasion of Kumara Purnima, a day when the moon is full, shining as though with pristine glory. For on this day only the young can rejoice, as the streets and lanes in this city are taken possession of, by young girls dressed in all their finery, their freshly washed hair loose on their shoulders, faces glowing in the warm clean light of the November sun. And one hears again the strains of a familiar tune in the air, the voice of nostalgia and abandon held in the chorus sung all over Orissa by unmarried girls:

> Oh this night of the full moon
> My long braids twined with *boula* blooms!

But, as I said earlier, nothing has been happening in this city where I have spent all my life. It is no longer the capital of Orissa. But there is an intimate air about the place, a simplicity of living which I never seem to find anywhere else. Often I sense a timeless image of life and death in the space around me, a something that touches me which comes from waters and hills, in the resigned and withdrawn houses lining the roads—where everybody lives, loves over and over again, and ultimately meets the evidence of what he has been living for, with a song that is no less than a hymn.

And yet, I feel so much has happened here since I was a child, when the savage tremor of an earthquake caught me unawares one afternoon almost seventy years ago. I remember the Cuttack of old; the embrace and shelter of a father's arms as he rushed me away from the house into the safe courtyard of the Nanda Deula to protect me from the tumbling buildings.

My romance with Cuttack has perhaps begun since that day. A new century has come into being. Today, we no longer live in the big building by the Kathjodi River. Then, the sprawling building where we lived was a boys' hostel, of which my father was the superintendent. The innumerable dark rooms, the long corridors, and the grounds in front were the world which shaped my childhood. There, I recollect, I used to wake up to the lingering bells of the Nanda Deula, to the haunting cries of egrets sweeping across the river, to the owl's hoot stretching out on the balcony on the upper floor toward the faraway stars. And there I learnt to live, intensely in my own way, exploring, imagining what lay beyond my safe little world. I asked myself my first questions: What is man's place in the universe? And what is my own place in it?

Now that I think of the Cuttack of years ago, I feel my place was with my father those early years, and that my Cuttack was built up through my father's eyes. It was then that I stood on the edge of the main road at Chandnichouk at dawn on *dasami*, and stared wide-eyed at the surging crowds, my little hand upraised, held fast in my father's. I remember now it was in the early morning hours that the *melana* took place, before the deities from different areas of the town were carried for the final immersion to the river, to the accompaniment of trumpets and beating of drums. It was then, for the first time, that I sensed something which seemed to make the heart run, toward a great adventure. In the sea of bodies, maybe something seemed to rise and fall, something that moved away from the passing deities as I watched, to reach out and touch me. The air was warm, the light of the occasion brilliant. And perhaps it was a mystery, the mystery of life that took me in, since then holding me a prisoner of my own experience, of both past and future.

Today the *melana* is held under cover of darkness, at night. There are, almost always, incidents of violence and rioting. But, I suppose, these can be attributed to the increasing numbers of people, and to the wild fervour which accompanies such festivities. Electricity and portable generators turn the city into an arena of many-splendoured light, as even dim corners of the city revel in defiant outbursts of light and sound. And sleep comes late to the inhabitants of Cuttack, almost at three in the morning. But I was speaking of Cuttack in late November. As I write this, Kali Puja and its accompanying festival of lights has ended, and also the festival of Bali Jatra on the south bank of the Mahanadi. The festival of Bali Jatra, which always seems trapped in an intense feeling of loss and nostalgia. At this time the past of Orissa comes alive, the glorious tradition of the ancient Oriyas, when Orissa was a proud and prosperous maritime nation, not the land we know today. It was this feeling which led me to write about this festival held on *Kartika Purnima* day:

> Childrens' voices break into the mist
> floating lazily over the river.
> Somewhere, too, float the voices
> of drowned men who open their eyes
> on the unknown bottom of the Mahanadi.
> Light silvers sand and water,
> an uncertain regret.
> The women are all there
> crowding the bank, women of my childhood,
> letting go their paper boats in the flow:
> frail wails of the Oriya race.
> And I live, with my words again,
> putting on a virtuous act
> to protect myself from the past:
> these men, valiant, lost,
> who appear in the mist with the rising moon
> where the unmistakable anguish
> of our sleep has gone.

As I walk again the streets, my gaze takes in the many changes that have taken place through the years. The city today has expanded beyond measure; a wide link road now brings the visitor into the city from the National Highway 5 passing over the road bridges on the Mahanadi and Kathjodi. The banks of both rivers have been reinforced, and a fairly wide road encircles the entire city. There is so much more concrete evident everywhere, and kilometres of asphalt: it is hard to envisage the city of my childhood. And still, amidst all these constructions, I seem to glimpse at times the soul of a forgotten empire: the heart that beats on as before inside the pitiful ruin of the vanquished fort of Barabati, and which fell to the British invaders last of all. A heartbeat, faint and primal, that can still be heard as one walks through the narrow, twisted lanes of Bania Sahi, where silversmiths keep on toiling at their exquisite creations of silver filigree through long hours. A soul, naked, human, that can be felt in the burning grounds of Satichoura and Khannagar, as the smoke of funeral pyres rises into the air and lies upon the young like a veil so they are unable to look into themselves and into the prism of death.

And as I continue to walk these streets today, and shall perhaps do so for the rest of my life that remains, I realise that I miss mainly the little things, the seemingly trivial happenings that made up the Cuttack or my boyhood. Maybe, most or all, I miss the tiny shack at the corner of the lane, where Duli Budhi used to sell her *pua* and *muan* at a pice a piece. I miss the wooden lamp-posts which held kerosene lamps with their warm and apprehensive light when I came back home in the evenings; I miss too the gnarled old banyans which stood like sturdy sentinels at the crossroads of Buxi Bazar, Mangalabag and Katakchandy, and where policemen stand today directing traffic. And miss also the horse drawn carriages that went by clippety clop on the uneven roads of those days.

But advancement is a sign of the times, and change is contained in life. I cannot hold anyone or my own nostalgia responsible for these deceptions of my heart.

Today, my father is no more. Duli Grandmother is dead. And so have many of my friends. I have more money than I ever had during my school or college days, when I could fill myself with a mere two annas. But I realise sadly that I can never buy the *puas* and *muans* of Duli Budhi even if I paid ten rupees a piece. It is late November, and my city grows older with each passing day, to reach another landmark. As I lie on the brink of dream and sleep, I know I shall get up on wintry mornings to feel simply the thick white mist on my face—this same mist of my childhood, so eloquent even today, and strain my ears to hear the oriole calls from the upper branches of the mango tree in our yard. And, gazing into the sunset waters of the Mahanadi and the Kathjodi, I shall let myself feel *that* unspoken sadness which lies below the surface, over and over again. And I know Cuttack shall not let me complain even if absence and longing rule the seasons of my life.

24

Stranger than Brothers: Writing at the Edge of Anonymity

At a recent grand gathering of academics away from India (in fact in the last week of August in Canterbury), and in which only a sprinkling of writers participated, I came across one of those light-headed questions that put me up against a wall once again. If I insist in saying that the question, or query, was in bad taste, I would not be wrong. But it has taken me quite a while to recover from the question's apparent innocuousness, and it merely pushes me to put the blame on my hypersensitivity to the common areas of understanding in our lives.

I will be truthful in narrating the basic bits of our conversation.

This academic who lives abroad and who is introduced to me by a common acquaintance at a coffee break between two sessions, asks me suddenly about a mutual friend who is a poet. His words go like this. "Do you know P.Q. Williams?" he asks (well, P.Q. Williams is of course a fictitious name I have deliberately substituted here). Our P.Q. is an important man in the realm of letters—especially Indian poetry. I reply enthusiastically, "Sure, he is a friend of mine." The academic's face takes on a different expression all of a sudden. His mouth twists in a sneer. He barks almost, for a reason most certainly known to him, and I can feel the shrapnel bursting from the small explosion somewhere in his head, "Friend? A friend in the way Pritish Nandy is a friend of PQ!"

I was taken aback by the words. It was only then that I realised that Pritish Nandy (this is the name the academic took) had taken this particular poet to task in one of his pieces on the state of writing in our country years ago, and apparently the academic hadn't forgotten about it. There is no need now to go into reasons or motivations for his sudden outburst. Obviously the academic is a good friend of PQ's. And that somehow he felt that the views expressed by Mr. Nandy were also shared by me; hence the unmistakable irony in his eruption.

Indeed, it was a light-hearted repartee. But the words speak for themselves. I could not help but be struck by them. Maybe I was being sensitive—something I should not have been. Still, the little episode narrows down the understanding of ourselves, and is one of the predicaments of a writer living among other writers in a traditional set-up such as ours. Something which comes to result in a loss of faith in a future for writing for a number of us.

Today, I live, as I have always lived, in a fairly remote corner of this large country, where our habits and attributes have not undergone any appreciable change through the years. Cuttack has always been a dirty, mosquito-infested town, hemmed in as it is between two rivers which almost invariably have flooded during the rainy months. Little has changed here; the people live still even as their fathers and their fathers' fathers had done before them, in spite of those modern conveniences the advent of technology has brought in. I grew up in such a set-up; my science training pushed me into a rational knowledge of the external world, fascinating me with ideas like the passionate whirl of electrons in apparently inanimate objects, by the intimations of mass and energy and their amazing coherence, with the coercion of a new light. And strangely, religion did not impose itself upon it. To me, science and religion were but bits of living, held in their own ways, securely in separate compartments. It seemed a safe arrangement, and it fooled me, as it fooled many others like myself, at least at an age when ambivalence does not seem to have much effect on the nature and wonder of life.

I never even dreamed then, that I would be some sort of a writer. The study of science had polarised my thinking; but, a shaky, unhappy childhood evidently tried to turn me around, and I felt the empty longing in each breath I took, as my breathing went on to mock me—and urged me to find escape in the rich world of books. Through those pages, impatient and restless, I discovered other eyes which did not leave mine; although the real world in which I lived callously looked on at me as I stood between an end and a beginning.

So I found myself going deeper into books. In a page I feel asleep. In a dream I offered myself, made love. In a page, a body of grace and mystery appeared before me, naked and trembling. And truth, which I hungered for.

And when I awoke, the words along the page were trembling still, like reeds along a shore.

I suppose my own writing began then, in my imagination. It was truly then that words began to have meaning—a meaning for life, long before I started writing in earnest. A meaning made up of seemingly opposites like pain and peace which are the true ingredients of the human condition, and eventually became the sign of my destiny, to be trusted as life progressed.

Only years later, when my initial attempts to write some fiction did not meet with any measure of success, and photography became too expensive an activity to be pursued seriously, did I turn to writing poetry. I was almost forty. My reading habits had developed enormously during the years; I consumed book after book of fiction, in English. The language had fascinated me since I was a child, my schooling had been through the medium of English, and it was only natural that I should use that medium for my struggling creative pursuits.

But it was later, when I had perhaps published my first book of poems (through a poet and not by some indifferent publisher), that I realised I had been writing in a language which my own people did not understand. Oriya was spoken around me, almost everywhere; but my limited Oriya vocabulary seemed an obstacle to my writing in my native Oriya. I had began to face a wall, even as I went on to publish book after book of poetry. A wall which I could not cross.

Even when my long poem entitled *Relationship* was published and selected for the Sahitya Akademi Award in 1981, nothing appeared to change. I was a writer, yes; but a writer of some other sort, of a different species, very un-Oriya. And here, *Relationship* was a long contemplation I had tried to build on the meanings of symbols on the stones of a crumbling, once-glorious Konarka temple. In twelve sections, the poem, fugue-like in construction, dealt with the mystery of suffering, with triumph and disaster of the Oriya psyche. And yet, the poem was not noticed in Orissa; or, if it was, was only read by a few of my own friends who believed in the seriousness of my poetic endeavours.

I was deeply disturbed. Hearsay accounts reached my ears, of how I did not 'belong' to the category of Oriya poets. I was writing in English, they said, and therefore my poetry could not be relevant to Orissa's cultural and social life. Even when, simultaneously with my own writing, I had been translating the works of Oriya poets, ancient and modern. I was alienated.

Today, after a number of years, the situation has not altered. Did I, or did I not, belong to the Oriya poetic tradition, I asked myself? I don't have any real answer to this. At times I find my eyes clouding with anger and sadness, held by my own impotence. But as a writer, I know that my poetry, although written in English, has not lost contact with the past. The land itself is a living presence for me, as are the old Oriya poets whose works I have read and admired.

This situation extends beyond the boundaries of Orissa. At meetings and at poetry festivals I have participated in throughout India, it has been this sense of estrangement that I have feared. One never desires to be marginal in such things; it is always the centre which pulls us, a centripetal urge. And perhaps all this divides the being we occupy.

But poetry, for me, helps one in finding oneself—in relation to the time he or she belongs to, to his era, or to separate himself from his other sleves. I realise it is difficult to 'share' our writing, because sharing is such a private thing. I suppose one can read a giant like Marquez, delight in his prose, marvel at the wide swings of imagination—but never can share the novelist's literature. Anyone who writes does so about the world he inhabits; the words are his own, his private ones, where he discusses the human condition he only knows.

Even then, this private world of the poet clamours secretly to be heard. There are many writers whom we never hear of, simply because they have stored away their words in their secret shelves. So many of my own friends write, but they have published little, and therefore remain unread. The reasons are many. But this is true: had their works been in print, maybe the world would have been richer to a certain extent.

Whom therefore, should we hold responsible for such a state of things? Our officials who hold prized positions in the arts with governmental organisations? Or the society we have built ourselves with our so-called civilised selves? I should like to ask: Doesn't society, the communities to which we belong, have any function toward artists? Shouldn't there be some form of support for talented writers and artists who, for lack of proper encouragement, lapse into lives of rejection, frustration and imposed silence? And, can we confidently state, that in the current polity, only the best writing will survive and come to stay?

I suppose the majority of our people will not agree if one asserts that society has a positive role to play for art and literature. And society includes the government. But the problems are especially complex for a country like ours, with its huge, illiterate population of almost seventy percent. A people like ours, who have always taken recourse to the oral tradition of culture, still find it hard to face the printed page. Perhaps the book, for them, helps to create the solitary intellectual, and causes the insufferable break between literature and life. I speak here from my own experience, my own existence as one living in the heart of a noisy bazaar in Cuttack. Across the old house where I live, a group of rickshaw-pullers gamble away, laughing out their impoverished lives through the warm afternoons. The woman who sells a brew called *cha* walks over with a small tumbler of *cha* at my call. I stand lazily at the gate, sipping the warm drink, as two five-year-olds pass by, see me and point upward, to the mango tree in our yard. The tree will only fruit in summer; there is still a long four months to go. The children reluctantly walk away. All of these are familiar faces, and yet there is a maw I am unable to cross. They have seen me with a book in my hand, and this knowledge of theirs has distanced me from them—I am identified as someone different, a scholar, maybe a writer. This is the crisis I face.

Added to this is the fact that art and literature are never what they once were. Even for the bare few who were attracted to literature and the arts, the twentieth-century world itself has changed, becoming reorganised, more complex. Readers, especially Indians, who have had the habit (a deplorable habit) of reading into literature certain moral and social values that have previously been read into Indian myth and history, find the new writing too abstract, disembodied and senseless. I don't know. I have myself experienced such criticism of my poems. Maybe the words and images I used were inconceivable to many. There are no poets writing today who can communicate with as large a number of readers as poets living earlier did in their time. And this applies to almost all the regional languages of India, with the possible exception of Urdu. To speak the naked truth, our readers are wary of finding alternative traditions besides the Ramayana.

So, for a writer, merely family and friends cannot serve as the support for his writing. It is indeed correct, that after the fifties, the government (both at the centre and in the states) has come up with forms of support—material support, in the manner of a fellowship or an award—but this, once again, has been seen somehow to go against the quality of writing as a whole. For instance, besides the tortuous exercise of identifying a truly meritorious work (among the many languages of India) for the dispensing of an award like the *Jnanapeeth*, and which in the end turns out to be probably a disputed bit of judgement, this very form of support becomes essentially a policy of recognition. Such a policy merely urges the granting of rewards for efforts that have already been made. And this only helps to put in order the writings of the immediate past, no more. What one needs, more than anything else perhaps, is not only to recognize, but to *discover* the writing for the future; and thus simultaneously helping to stimulate new writing and present it for various readers.

Another outcome of these awards, and something which cannot be refuted, is the growing careerism in poetry. There seems to be a fantastic abundance of poets writing today—those who believe that their need to write is *not* as great as their need to be read. In other words, these people want to be known as poets. Writing has always been a secret process of hard labour; and a poem only evolves in the privacy and isolation of oneself. Perhaps the only way to *be* a poet is to keep on writing; and not to abandon the need to write, irrespective of publication. It is a pity that many among such careeristic poets publish a lot, corresponding with other poets, use today's public relation methods, most of them with an eye for an academy award. For a true poet, however, writing itself becomes a force of silence in this discipline he practises.

There is no doubt that the reading public are beneficiaries of the writing practised by our poets and novelists. They, therefore, should be aware of their responsibilities—trying in ways to ensure that works of literature are read, circulated, and ultimately preserved for future generations. Public and private philanthropies are needed, because they will influence the quality of writing available to us.

And, on the other hand, one feels that one should not make too much of literature, or of art in general. It is not right to make a piece of writing into a deity, to be put on a pedestal, to be worshipped. One asks: Has the book-culture paralysed us (the serious intellectual) to such an extent that any other medium of communication seems false?

Of late, one notices that the changing habits of the new rich have gone on to deviate the traditional patterns of Indian culture. Side by side, we are also witnessing a monstrous regional chauvinism, which might turn writing itself to a cancerous growth. At a time when there are no longer any generally-accepted standards of poetic taste, these creations will take on different forms—which have to be sifted and redefined in the years ahead.

Finally, I should like to ask myself: What is my role in this changing literary landscape? The effect of my poems, if at all, even after years of writing, has been minimal. From ten readers of my poems I had ten years ago, perhaps the number of readers has increased to thirty. I don't say this with a sense of frustration. If I have spoken of any ideas on my poetry—on food and shelter, on such basic necessities that still plague my people, which I have seen myself in the remote interiors of Orissa—what good have these ideas of mine done?

Today, I feel that the reasons for the growing separation between the serious writer and the potential reader can be pinned down to the Indian academic and critic. It is mainly he who never fails to speak of the mystically inherent character of the Indian mind whenever he discusses a book. True that mystery is one of the essences of art. But all this talk of the "Indian sensibility" in our writing only helps to sustain the academic's own idea of nationalism. And many of our writers, by responding rather innocently to such statements, only contribute in complementing the academic on his own importance.

In a time of increasing parochialism in our writing, our real offender is the academic. He is the all-knowledgable critic, book-reviewer, essayist, anthologist and purveyor of schools of thought. His ego has been tolerably well attended to.

25

Land to Land: A Moon in Our Eyes

A journey to another country is often a journey of exploration. Although this statement is more true for the general traveller, it is also fairly true for a writer of one country visiting another—even to meet with other fellow-writers and to visit other writing "habitats". I refer to a generalisation which is not restricted to the literal meaning of exploration. Yet in a way it is. My recent visit to the USSR as a guest of the Union of Soviet Writers, was, to all accounts, the scene of a private exploration.

When one has lived most of one's life in the country of one's birth, the sudden change, both in place and time, helps to indentify the person to his or her own self in a way one had never experienced before. This is especially valid for a writer. One tends to see oneself in a new perspective, from the dimensions of a different world, in the new coordinates of an unfurled imagination. As a writer, one feels the forces working upon oneself, and one experiences a pull along a direction not yet formed in one's mind, but vague and changing. Perhaps the writer's imagination could be said to waver, seeking allegiance not only to the writer's own country, but in some inexplicable manner to the country he now finds himself in—all this which he finds hard to explain to himself.

My imagination as an Indian is but natural that it be rooted in India, where I have lived most of my life except for brief visits abroad. This sense of belonging, to the Indian earth (in my case, to the coastal Orissa countryside), to its very different social, cultural and religious milieu, has led to certain ideas and convictions which become mine, and which have, in turn, helped to *make* my poems and stories. Many of my poems (truthfully, my better poems) are built around my place; rather, within the place itself. This fact, both consciously and unconsciously, helps to polarise my imagination, to let me live in the manner I want to live, to determine my dreams, and to explore finally my inner self. For only in this way I feel I can be more honest with myself—because I try to write about the air, water and blood in my immediate surroundings, about time and space which float up from the marshy green paddies of this land and touch me, of the ancient temple bell that creates its enchanted distance in my mind, and of the strange and sad country of ruined temples which has been my home. Thus if I say that it is to Orissa that I owe my poetry, I would not be wrong. For it is Orissa which creates the joy and the hurt and the grief I cannot do without. And hence my poetry. In an early short poem, I said:

> Stone cuts deep
> A bell trembles,
> touched by the pain
> of countless people
> Across the temple square
> the wind
> that settles on my shoulders
> has nowhere to go:
> neither a silence
> nor an answer

and even today I do not know whether I am more aware or not. With the passing of years perhaps there has come to be an educated clarity of introspection in my recent poetry, but it is difficult to say whether my heightened self-awareness has led me to any complete "answers".

It was Nietzsche who wrote that philosophy has always been "the personal confession of the author and a kind of involuntary and unconscious memoir." And perhaps all art and literature deals with this, trying to build a personal memoir that would be objective enough to reach toward the universal. So from a little acre of native soil emerges a kind of faith urging one to write about it; and in this way one tries to follow the very many writers who have spoken so marvellously about their individual places of existence; then perhaps to go on and on in our separate endeavours never to exhaust it.

To my mind comes immediately the novels of Lev Tolstoy: *War and Peace, Resurrection, Anna Karenina. War and Peace* was written by Tolstoy no doubt; but when I think about it now, I'd like to assert that this great novel could only have been written by a Russian. It is a novel rooted in the Russian milieu as no other work seems to be; for in the book throbs the thought and world of Russia of those bygone days: "it creates a world after its own image." I could go on to cite examples of such works everywhere, which, though remaining rooted in their own environments, transcend their boundaries and touch distant souls like mine...

When Alexander Blok wrote,

> Over the Black Sea and the White, and on
> into black nights and into white days
> wildly a rigid face stares from the dark unknown,
> Tartar eyes into the dark unknown haze...
> Ember-red over your camp every evening
> there is a silent continual glow...
> Flickering dream-mirage, why are you signalling?
> Why do you toil with my free soul so?

wasn't he simply speaking out his mind about his country, Russia? And of his own vision—a Russia perhaps feathered by an Asia of his own imagination?

Maybe this is what I meant when I stated that we, as writers, like to stay close to the scene of our life. This is what each poet does, building a silence that encloses him. This is what Ivan Drach does when he writes:

> I am a form out of zinc. I contain
> heavy pellets...

creating a silence of knowledge, and the poet waits for that silence to explode, ultimately to become a poem. But what is this silence of which the poet himself is in fear, as he waits inside of it?

Is it a wet crushed jasmine in the rain, a half-forgotten tune, the plaintive call of an oriole in a faraway tree; or is the silence the shut, submissive eyes of an outcaste girl being stoned to death for making love to a Brahmin youth? Or does it lie in the screams of a girl being raped in the dark rainy night of Cuttack, or in the terror in a young girl's face as she runs naked along a napalm-bombed road in Vietnam? Or in the whimper of an infant buried alive for a week under the rubble in earthquake-hit Mexico City?

Whatever it be, it is this silence which imprisons the poet, so that he realises he can never be free; and he knows he can never be where he finds himself. Today, as I write this, I am strangely kept awake by the roar of the crowds in the escalators of the Tretyakovskaya Subway Station, although I am in reality far far away from Moscow, in my house in a dusty rural Cuttack street. But sights and sounds of another world darken the outlines of my dreams, and at times imagination fuses into reality until it is difficult to distinguish one from the other. Or here, back in my homeland, I have an image of myself standing on the firm earth of six hundred winters, listening intently to the melodious chimes of Suzdal, and wrestling secretly with the weight of unknown presences.

And this is probably what I had in mind when I began this epistle, viz., that a visit to another country becomes a journey of exploration. Exploration, yes; but decidedly different from what and how a tourist feels when he is there. For the poet begins to create a place or scene to which he can emotionally relate; and enveloping the poet so totally that he is carried along by the intensity of the moment to build his poem:

> Great wings extend
> from the Flame to the martyrs.
> Crows are restless,
> a baby in a crib looks up
> at the light.
> It is beginning to rain.
> Memories are silent,
> nothing answers.
> And the flowers sold
> by old ladies in the marketplace
> still reveal
> their blood-stained feathers.

These lines make up a poem I wrote in Lvov, in the west of Ukraine, close to the Polish border. It was the sight of the ever-burning flame to the martyrs of World War II, the sight of boys and girls changing guard in the rain, the old women selling flowers in the marketplace combined with thoughts in my mind of the War-dead that brought about the poem.

Having written the poem, I ask myself: Is it a good poem? I do not know. I do not know whether it is a poem at all. I only know that the poem came about—haunted perhaps by the spilt blood during the war—when I was there in Lvov, far far away from my own land. But why, I cannot say.

As a writer today, I cannot, do not pretend righteousness. Only this I am sure of—that a writer should, first of all, be honest to himself and to his readers. I should like my poems to be a testament to this. And this is what I'd like to be.

26

The Door

I sit in a Sunday-morning emptiness, waiting for nothing. It is the beginning of another year; but nothing, once again, is quite dead and finished with. It is simply that I have surrendered to this rite of a year's beginning—this magic space in which one lives for a moment, holding one's breath in some measure of wonder, thinking of what a new time could create. I emerge from my mindless thinking, the leftover of a year gone, drinking in the mild sun of January. But, as I said, the weight of my own reason-ruled days presses upon me. Perhaps I am somehow eager to separate what looked real from what wasn't. My eyes search the air, but all I can see are people moving listlessly down the road, hear the barking of a stray pariah dog. I realise that I have not changed my skin while the year passed by; I am no more devil or angel that I was before. I am neither a snake nor a bird; my voice is the same, but it no longer hisses nor is melodious. And, I have still not been able to take up the halo of faith which I had thought one day I would; I have only gone along with what any day would ask of me. Nothing else, but the day perhaps, standing over my shoulder, waiting.

The time of the new year is here. It contains me, as does this room in which I sit, savouring this Sunday-morning emptiness. It is plainly ridiculous to think that this time will shut out the old year, and all that goes with it, even the years which have gone before. All those years which go on to make up this consciousness of the present. And my memory fills with what happened and what didn't. As if anything could ever end. Like one's birth, and then, that small miracle called childhood;

childhood, which lets life in, without asking what life wants from it.

My childhood has a door hidden in its dark inside. I know I cannot escape it. It comes back to me again and again, this door, shutting behind me. Just as any door does, opening a little before it shuts again.

A long time it has been in my life, this door I am talking about. During those first years which matter as nothing else does later. And my door was the front door of the house in which we spent our early years in Cuttack. This door, which was set into a brick wall that went round our small courtyard. Painted black, the two halves of the door fitted into a sort of wooden frame, but which never locked into place when the two halves were closed. A small iron chain was fixed to the outer side of the door, and one had to pull this chain to skip it over an iron rung. A lock was then attached to the rung to secure the door.

Today my mind is that drab, ghostly old house sometimes I come to visit. As time once more does not appear real. Fifty years ago to this day, I was left to myself, to live in that house with the pitch-painted front door. I recollect that our house, which was located at the end of a narrow lane, was surrounded by tall deodar trees and a few coconut palms. But most of all, what buries me inside myself even today is the thought of the wind in the evenings, blowing in from the south-west, particularly during the monsoon, which lasted a long four months from the beginning of June till early October.

It was the wind, yes, which played its havoc on me in my empty room with the four bare walls. And on the door of which I speak, as it kept rattling in the wild wet wind. I was a child then, a mere boy, growing up, held by rules and laws which my mother did not hesitate to enforce upon me.

Mother never left me to myself. Studies were, of course, my main purpose in life, with most of the day which I spent at school; but the rest was set to a strict schedule by her. My father was away, working as a Sub-Inspector of Schools in the remote Orissa countryside, and there was only my younger brother for company in the home. No one else lived with us in those days, and my sister hadn't been born. As the eldest in the house, I had to look after the household chores, besides doing my regular homework. It was my responsibility to close and open the front door at dusk and dawn; my duty to open the door to visitors when they came and knocked at all odd hours. And on top of everything else, lay the shadow of Mother, who seemed to be always at my heels. The rigid discipline coupled with her false accusations for reasons she only knew, stifled me at times. I was totally unhappy.

My hours in the house became a sort of constant torment, subjected as I was to the whims of Mother. There did not seem to be any way out. I was too timid, too cowardly those early years, but I did harbour thoughts of running away from home. I only wished my father was there—instead of those brief, infrequent visits when he came home on leave to Cuttack.

So there was this door which stayed on in my mind, a thing which shut me off from the outside world when I returned home after school. The war had begun, the Second World War; and I was about eleven, perhaps twelve. I recollect we had very little time to play after school gave over, except during the summer months; and Mother always insisted that the front door should be shut before darkness fell. Alone in the house, with my kid brother and an ill mother, I suffered the fear and apprehension of living in a fairly large house. I felt my face, soft and lonely, lying awake at night; not knowing how I would protect the family if some danger came our way. And added to the emptiness of the house, was the dismal soughing of the wind among the encircling deodars—made more fearful by the daily blackout which had been strictly enforced at night. We did not have electricity in the house, and had to use shades on the oil lamps to prevent the light showing in the dark. All this made me suffer the fear of being abandoned, of being trapped in a place which was not of my making. The gloom was intolerable.

Often alone, I think of this door of my childhood which served both as a refuge from the terrors of the outside world, and as an object which mutely went on to lock me in, offering me no escape. It became both a haven and a prison; and my mind positioned itself both inside and out. Perhaps the doors of all houses, everywhere, do just that. There is always something very final, very secretive about doors—a feeling from which it is difficult to get away.

My memory does not seem to fail me today. Perhaps it never will. I know I will always feel the door, this door of my uncomfortable childhood until my death, until my consciousness is there. The ugly door, which did not lock into place in those days, and does not even today, half a century later—but served its purpose of locking me in, and locking the world outside too.

Behind my door, within the walls of my own room and of my own mind, my breath moves in circles today. I keep wondering about it, but the door has put in enough fear inside me, so that I cannot bridge past and future, good and evil, anymore.

But what is this door of which I have been speaking? Is it the image of myself I see in the mirror at times, when my left hand becomes the right, and my right eye becomes my left? Or is it the shadow of myself, which I feel powerless to shake off however much I try? Or is it the freedom I can never possess, which I do not remember to have had since my childhood, a freedom my mother severely bound, and which appears today to be more and more a parody of death? Or is it something that will not let me return to the world I love, and which lies beyond all understanding?

Sometimes my door is a shadowy shape in spring moonlight, when the fragrance of mango blossoms flits in the air; at times seductive, at times proud, as I see it float away, like a bit of my existence, homeless, like the cry of a March koel—on a sea of regret and sorrow, of tenderness and loss.

And it makes me ask myself: Is it the same door, on the other side of which I have stood and waited innumerable times when I was a child, for someone to come and open it, so that I could enter?

But, suddenly, all is silence. My mind contains me, as does this room where I live today, and contains my ageing body. I can sense the door's presence in the shadows on the walls, in the photographs I have hung on the walls with care, in the eyes of Einstein which look up at me from beneath the glass sheet on my writing desk. I can sense the bones of the door in the words of the poems I have written through the years, and strangely begin to feel the weight of this framework of bone I am carrying within me.

Somehow the door's power has entered me, I know, and I am afraid of its pride.

But why does this door keep me waiting even now? As it kept that pretty cousin of mine waiting years and years ago, when she used to rap on the door in desperation and fear to prevent herself from being beaten by her drunk husband on many evenings? And when, as a boy of twelve perhaps, I used to tread on my shadow in apprehension as I took slow steps in the darkness to open the door and let her in?

Today I feel relieved I don't live in that house. I left it long back, seeking a kind of freedom from the tyranny the rules of my mother had imposed upon me. I live in the same town of Cuttack, but elsewhere, right in the middle of a crowded bazaar where traffic ceases only at midnight.

And I don't wish to shut the door of my room where I spend my time. Open, somehow my room brings in the earth into me, and opens my mind. The earth comes right in, and with it the sky; a tune floats into my head, some unknown melody I do not seem to have heard before. And there is a strange movement in the air, arising out of all the stillness....

Maybe this whole story of my door is an unreal one. In this silence of Sunday, I hear the noises of death, through the sound of the opening of the door from which I thought I had moved away. It is hard for me to say why this door keeps on coming over and over again in both my waking life and in dream; and why it keeps on pervading the poems I have written through the years.

I should like to reproduce here a short poem I did many years back, and which appeared in *Critical Quarterly* for the first time in the Summer 1974 issue:

> This thing
> wakes me like a hand
>
> Grass waits

And rock
takes the wind's place

Huge door
drifting
with feet of light

My eyes quietly open
before the night's

I titled the poem, "The Door". I don't wish to go into the feelings that made the poem. But whatever the door may mean to me today, must have had its roots in that door of my childhood home: that perimeter, which had its own gravitational field—and which contained my mother, my younger brother, my always absent father—and also held the pain of carrying my mind in front of me like a decapitated head.

Today, my father is dead. Mother lives in the same old house as she did when Father was alive. But I moved away from the house of my childhood to live by myself. The surroundings of my old house are no longer the same; new houses have come up around it, in place of the cluster of palms and deodars. But whenever I am there, I seem to hear the wind in the branches of the now-absent trees, and the fruit-bats squabbling high up somewhere, and the hooting of an owl, faraway and yet so near.

And the door: it's still there, a silent sentinel of years I have left behind. I have deliberately tried to move it away, by moving away myself, but have not come out from exile. Here in my own room, in this newer emptiness of this house, something keeps moving. I don't know what. But I cannot purge myself of that jungle, of that wasteland, where a bit of my childhood knocks still on that dark-faced door in stubborn silence.

27

Hedging the Heart: To What is the Poet Responsible?

Without doubt we are living in troubled times. Ours is a time of great upheaval; and I'd like to believe we suffer mainly from a crisis of faith, if we set aside wars and revolutions. We wonder whether the twentieth century will be looked back upon as a time of barbarism, the beginner of a new dark age, or will it be one of those times of chaos, a crucible where a new and more creative world was being formed? Difficult questions these. As we enter 2001, the outlook seems dim. We suffer a sense of loss of orientation. Our little garden patch has become a world fraught with tension. The answer, for a person like me, who would like to call himself a poet, seems to be retreat, or escape and regression. And this can only come about through something like my writing, these poems I would want to write.

Today, as we face the anonymity of urban life and the new freedoms of a more permissive society, our needs appear to change. Our desires too, shaped by the aggressive media of communication. Still, the same questions will haunt the poet; those questions which have apparently no answers, and about which poets have written and asked themselves at all times. And because life is reminiscence, our poetry too is reminiscence. This memory, this terrible sepulchre which we have inherited, and carry inside us, will not leave one alone, ever. And the poet will ask: Who is that child crying, why, without a mouth? Alongwith that eternal equation of rich and poor, the splintered dilemma of day and night, of peace and war. Can poetry ever help to solve it? Can poetry ever turn the world and the workings of the world into song?

A question I would like to ask myself is: If poetry makes us more conscious of the essence of our day-to-day existence, of life's complexities and meaning, does it have an effect upon action, even political action? One would confirm that this is a very old idea: and that one cannot deny the truth of the statement that there is an eventual effect on our actions, whether social or political. And if poetry may influence politics, we could say (extrapolating things) that poetry is politics, and so this poetry is not poetry at all, it is just not good for anything.

But is it right that we blame the poets of our time when society goes wrong? When people begin to argue that we have failed to defend the principles of social and political democracy—the result of the apathy or callousness of responsible classes of society, which makes up our writers? Or more particularly our poets, whose accountability is the purity of language and who supposedly represent the class of writers at its noblest? If I limit my ideas to the poetry around me, the poetry I am familiar with, such as Indian English poetry, the poetry in Oriya by our recognised poets, and a little of Bangla and Assamese poetry, would I be wrong if I concluded that our poets are encased in a private world of their own invention, where they cultivate certain delusions: for example, their superiority to practical life, the belief in the autonomy of their poetry, and their innermost desire to resist change formally, intellectually and emotionally. I make these remarks from my own, rather polarized observations, familiar as I am with the poetry produced both in English and Oriya, this poetry which contains, and reveals in, the abundance of self. The dilemma of narcissism, of too much self, I should think, deviates from the direction of true poetry that should find a sense of relation between self and other, the inner and outer world, the personal and social worlds. John Berger, in *The Success and Failure of Pablo Picasso*, writes perceptively about this dilemma of modern artists. I like to quote:

> they are far away and unseen—so that at home most people are protected from the contradictions of their own

> systems: those very contradictions from which all development must come.

Many of our poets, primarily those poets who live in a bureaucratic or academic world of their own, elevate the artist to the ethereal, where we deny the connections between self and other, separating language from social relations. (Once again, one asks, is this an Indian trait?) We revere this isolated human being (our artist, our poet) and treat his imagination as something he has inherited, a gift from God, as though there were no logical relationship, or historical relationship between the self and the world. We are then aware that we write without any real sense of community or audience. It would be right to cite instances of Indian English poets who are "exiled" from India by their own choosing, preferring to live in the United States or Canada or Europe. For such a poet or artist, what would his difficulties be? Perhaps, humanly, he would, certainly be very lonely. But what will this loneliness mean to his or her art? It will mean he or she will begin to write nostalgically about the country he (she) abandoned, or maybe demean the social values he (she) grew up with. Later on, he is sure to run out of subjects or themes. He might not run out of emotion or feelings but he will, I feel, run out of subjects to hold them.

That is why the poetry of such Indian English poets fails, even if their poetry is praised by reviewers and readers here and in the West. Clearly the great poets of Latin America and Eastern Europe live *inside history*, as is the case with our poets writing in their respective regional languages, and their imaginations are vitalised by that deeper perspective. In comparison Indian English poetry appears lifeless, stuck in the mire of intimacies, without the arms of history and tradition. For such significant poetry to be produced, we would have to create our poetry out of the ashes of our culture, both Indian and colonial British. And we have to cultivate the relationship between the social and the personal in order to give that positive momentum to poetry. One is afraid though, that such writing could bring in a measure of self-consciousness to it because of a loss of moral poise. Perhaps, again, it is difficult for me to write such poetry. Still, this is the poetry I would want to write—even when I am aware that such a poetry is not accepted (dismissed as a matter of fact) by poets who follow the British poetic tradition, where craftmanship seems all.

I should like to confess here that I began to write poetry in English simply because I could use English easily to express myself. Perhaps that isn't right for a poet, I do not know. But I have always thought of myself as an Oriya poet who, *incidentally* writes in English. And today, with five collections of Oriya poetry, I am not sure whether I could be labelled an Indian English poet.

A poem I'd like to quote in full and which resulted from my periodic visits to the starvation-affected region of Kalahandi in my state, and which perhaps suffers from an impatient self-consciousness because of this bridge between the social and personal is titled "Deaths in Orissa":

> Faces of tree-bark and grief
> hang against God's hand in the world
> that cannot lift itself up to help.
> In the corners of women's eyes
> the rainbow breaks against the sunrise.
>
> Nothing but the paddy's twisted throat
> exposed on the crippled bleak earth,
> nothing but impotence in lowered eyes,
> nothing but the tightening of the muscles
> in Bhagyabati's neck which her outcast mother
> would herself have liked to throttle to death,
> nothing but the cries of shrivelled women
> cracking against the bloodied altar of Man,
> nothing but the moment of fear
> when they need a God who can do them some good.
> Oh I am a poet who barks like a dog.
> Open the window, I say, so I can breathe.
> Let not my memory be like a tiger in ambush.
> But there is this dangerously alive body
> and only a lathi or knife can tear it apart.

This might not be a good poem, craftwise. But it came out of my own experience. And it was an honest attempt of mine. But what I'd like to clarify is, that it came from my own justification to *think*.

Eliot, however, with his stance of resigned defiance, was often against the idea of the poet as thinker. In his words: "In truth neither Shakespeare nor Dante did any real thinking—that was not their job." What appears as thought in a poet is no more than the emotional equivalent of thoughts prevalent in his time. As far as poetry is concerned whether these thoughts were part of a great philosophy or not is indifferent, so long as they express some permanent human impulse. At the same time poetry should have the freedom to express in any way appropriate to it the diversity of human experience. We may take this further to say that a poet is responsible to his conscience, to his sense of what is right and wrong, to that retinal image focussed by both knowledge and judgement. It is difficult for one to locate the relation of poetry to social action: this has never been done perhaps; so it is not possible to define what that relation is. But this is true: that poetry has some effect upon conduct, in so far as it affects our emotions. To what extent then, is the poetry, say, of someone like Gajanan Muktibodh, an effect?

Poetry has the right to judge. One feels one has the right to make such a statement. Poets, writers and artists especially. One can infer that our right to judge is fed by the obsequious ways of our politicians, who must ingratiate themselves with a mass electorate. This is evident because our public men may think and feel like the emperor Aurangzeb, but there are none who would talk like him in front of their public audiences. Poets, probably, watch the game of politics from the sidelines. We are spectators, when we are poets; not players. Although the view from the sidelines enables us to see clearly much that is blurred to the players, it also distorts vision in certain ways. The spectator easily assumes toward the players an attitude of condescension, inclining toward disdain. Our poet here, is the spectator we are speaking about.

A great danger we encounter, as poets, away from direct participation in the affairs of the community, is that we take ourselves easily as the guardians of moral purity. I could say: Politics are dirty and the government is a fraud: but I, as a poet, am clean, my aims honourable. I have better things to do than politics, and no time to waste on plotters and schemers. Politics can only distract me from those better things, remove me from the better people who do those better things, and probably splash me with mud and blood in the end. So let a poet not be snug in his belief that he is the upholder of his society's (or of his country's) morals. This is wrong. Let not this vanity lead to a sort of ranting, a protest that could ultimately veer him away from the true poetry that is his goal. In one of my own poems, there are three lines which say:

> Any time my Government breaks its promises,
> a line of this poem
> is dragged along the wide, clean streets of New Delhi...

Maybe this is an example of what I referred to, i.e., of my stand as a guardian of moral behaviour. In stating this I do seem to suffer from a small sense of guilt—a guilt that our educated middle class carry with them when they go on to criticise the Government for whatever ails our people. And yet, no world would perhaps exist unless poetry (out of all the arts) creates it for us. And this poetry has its source within *every* person who lives.

So I don't think it would be out of place to say that the poet who doesn't see what is happening around him is dead; and the poet who *only* sees reality around him is *also* dead.

The poet who is only irrational will only be understood by himself and his closest friend or lover, and this is very sad. The poet who is *all reason* will even be understood by fools, and this is also terribly sad. So poetry will not stand by hard and fast rules, by good and evil: but it will be there, and cannot be defeated.

In the end, two alternatives come to mind when one thinks of the responsibility of poets. First, is it right to put such a burden on a man of imagination and dreams, on a poet? And secondly, is there no other class of individuals (I should say, intellectuals like scientists, philosophers and statesmen) who might also be held responsible?

Poetry is a deep, inner calling in man; from it came liturgy, the vedas and psalms, and the content of religions. The poet confronted nature's phenomena and in the early ages called himself a priest, to safeguard his vocation. In the same way, to defend his poetry, the poet of the modern age accepts the honour from the masses. Today's social poet is still a member of the earliest order of priests. In the old days he made his pact with darkness, today he must speak and interpret the light.

28

By the Way

What should a poem be? Or a poetry book be? I still don't know, even after thirty-five years of continuous writing, day after day.

For me, each poem has been a painful struggle. Each poem has been an exploration, of an idea or a subject; which I thought would hopefully shine with coherence and truth when I was writing the poem. Unfortunately it has not been so.

Life and art are closely linked. And yet, somehow, both do not flourish at the same time. When the demands on life are there, all art (literature included) takes a back seat. The greater the demands on life, the more unnecessary seems art. Art, then, becomes a frill which can be kept out.

When these demands on life are present, what one says matters—because literature is at the service of social justice or revolution. One has only to know how to do this. For a writer is judged then by *what* he says than *how* he says it.

Ernest Hemingway once said that his first commitment as a writer was to the truth. In other words, everything, even truth, must be given up to serve the cause of social justice. Were his readers convinced? This might make literature vulnerable, the danger of it degenerating into propaganda. At the same time, T.S. Eliot insisted that meaning was an element of form—which implies that a work of art should be judged by *how* it is said and not *what* it said.

So what does one do, torn between such contradictory notions? I do not know. But it is true that Eliot's ideas did a lot of damage to writing everywhere.

A serious writer is therefore left to find for himself that balance in which important truths express themselves with clarity and coherence.

How does one achieve *that* balance?

Or, should one try to write the sort of poetry common readers would like to read?

29

Silence: Poetry's Last Word

Poetry makes me write poems with a bad heart. I don't know what that exactly means, but it is the heart that makes one turn secretly into someone—a leader or loser perhaps—pushing one to choose values, attitudes, and to do the not-so-obvious; this heart, as it keeps on trying to hide the wounded walls of its house, and at the same time asking itself for a meaning to our lives.

Somewhat hesitatingly, one feels, after years of writing, that one should give up the notion of writing poetry altogether, because this alone is what we know: that they, the words, the makers of poetry, will forever remain beyond us in spite of ourselves and our painstaking attempts to let the poems we have created tell us we would be happy with them.

Maybe one can understand this inclination of not wanting to write at some point of space and time better if one considers a recent piece from the life of a writer I have highly admired and respected. Around the middle of 1984, the blind writer Jorge Luis Borges said in an interview: "I haven't even burned any books except my own, which don't count, nor have I built any walls either." What exactly had Borges in his mind when he said this? Had he suddenly become aware that all his writing was futile at that moment? Or, had he lost all respect for the dreams he had for man? Nevertheless, Borges also wrote an essay called "The Wall and the Books" in which he wrote about Shih Huang Ti, the first emperor of China, and said that the emperor destroyed history, destroying all books before he became emperor.

It appears therefore, that at some point of time there is an inexplicable urge to build that wall, which could well mean the feeling of *not* writing at all; or perhaps the breaking down of some hazy dream or a reality of the poet's own making: like watching the flash of the knife the poet holds slice into one of the heads of this double-headed snake called poetry. And yet if neither is real, does it make any difference at all?

At the start, I talked of a "bad heart" fully well realising that the meaning of that term was unclear. It is true, however, that morality, as it is understood in the general way, was not in my mind when I referred to that expression, in the way both good and evil are. Bad or good, these terms are always postulates, never absolutes. And in vagueness I have felt the sense of that "bad heart" in day-to-day encounters in my own life, along the many directions life takes me. At the same time it's an indisputable fact that my judgements suffer. One's own responses are shaped by a number of factors, and it is difficult to be objective, whatever that word might mean. A commonplace example could point to that moment when I (not anyone else) get a "bad heart".

When I have watched with my heart advertisements on national television and seen film and sports celebrities extol the qualities of some suiting or fabric, with the camera panning in wide sweeps to reveal the plush interiors of a lavish lifestyle, I will admit I experience a twinge of sadness; when, I suppose, I should have been taken in by the sheer magnificence of such living. Perhaps this is what I would call giving one a "bad heart". That such an inconsequential thing, which is of no significance whatsoever, would trigger a response of uneasiness, seems hard to explain. Is this sense of guilt intensely felt, especially for one who lives in a country like ours where almost half the people are hungry and impoverished? Feelings like these, waxing and waning in the blur of the mind, help in focussing on oneself, placing the person at some point of time and meaning. And poetry, the process of writing it, does just that. The reasons are all there. They are there because man is able to think. Or simply because man has this hidden core of a conscience which he finds he cannot entirely subjugate or ignore.

Poetry has always been responsible to life. By this, one means that a poet, is first of all responsible to his or her own conscience, otherwise he or she cannot be called a poet. And maybe the other factors necessary to the makings of a good poet, will only come later. These may ordinarily imply the craft, or the language the poet will use with skill in his poems. But somehow, these appear as frills in a poem that is already full with feeling, because the poem would have already done what it was meant to do; in other words, touch another human being, before one came to notice the other qualities of the poem.

And so, if the poet's inner voice matters, it seems but natural that he would write about those things which appear unfair to him. It is the poet again who will talk about injustice and cruelty and greed in a society in which he lives, hoping in his heart of hearts that these would be taken care of. Certainly one cannot place the poet in the category of a social reformer; but there can be no denying the fact that he would like to see a just and fair society come into existence, to see that smile appear on the face of every destitute child on the street, on every man, woman and animal on this earth he inhabits.

But these are tall orders. History has always proved otherwise.

The outcome is that the poet uses his "bad heart" to go on writing his poems until he comes to a stage when he would perhaps make the ultimate decision in his life: *not* to write. This will only come about through years of painful indecision and work, through countless words which he had supposed would get the attention they deserved. It is like a wall he faces at this moment, as he waits with anxious breath to cross his literary Rubicon.

It is the poem one writes, or, the series of poems one writes in one's lifetime that pursue one throughout his life. I believed once, perhaps when I began writing poetry, that the poem behaved as an act of exorcism, helping one to 'cleanse' oneself; or, as I said earlier in this piece, to make a better heart the poet possessed. Today, after a lot of thought, one experiences the sense of being pursued, perhaps hunted, by the poems one has made. The poems act as surprises, at times amazing one, bringing the deeper, inner silence of a sentient being into focus. So perhaps the poem, with its words, triggers an inner silence and in the end shakes one.

A poem doesn't take the poet on the path to knowledge, as is commonly supposed. He or she never becomes a reformer of the world, never a philosopher. The poet doesn't lift himself onto a pedestal of learning. On the other hand, he is driven by longing, driving large words with this longing that overwhelms him. Because, plainly speaking, longing is all the poet has.

Our very own Rabindranath Tagore wrote some of the briefest lyrics in his later life as he moved toward a silence he could only conceive. Lyrics which were pared and honed to a centre of consciousness as never before, stripped of many of the traditional elements of his earlier style; yet containing that profoundness of thought which makes poetry rise above itself:

On the shore of the western sea
the day's last sun
voiced its last question
in the stillness of dusk:
Who are you?

There was no answer.

(Trs. mine)

An enigmatic silence lies behind these lines. Is this what every serious poet moves forward to? Perhaps. It represents a very crucial period in the writer's lifetime. And if we ask ourselves the question: What is it that has precipitated this state of mind, so that one's whole output seems superfluous, useless too the struggle and urge of an entire life? Is it only his bad heart that has motivated him? Is it a mere feeling of guilt that tries to lead him into a state of self-effacement, of himself and his work? A basic need to humble himself at a point of time when he is able to observe his own self in relation to his surroundings—something he has ignored so far in his desire to build himself as a significant writer of our time?

So, the silence. A silence of inevitability which could be more eloquent, more meaningful to the writer of words.

It is easy to find instances in our own century of writers who chose not to write after being completely successful in the one or two books they published. The American novelist, J.D. Salinger, is one whose silence after a remarkable literary feat remains open to question. But it is a silence one does not need to go into, or try to understand. I should like to believe that the silence was of Salinger's own making, a silence that served his needs of life and which his words were unable to fulfil. Maybe it is like a ride inside a deep night, when one is never alone, but finds his being in the darkness and in the wind's rush. Or in something that contains that distant intelligence of a voice he has not heard before.

Yet there could be a number of reasons for bringing about this kind of negative desire in a writer. It is not mere apathy. Nor is it some chemistry. The mind makes a symbol of nothing. It is a real need the writer feels. On the other hand, we have to acknowledge that some writers are driven by a belief that their work will one day be known and appreciated. But many more must finally conclude that their struggle and pain in such an unwelcome obscurity is certainly not justified. These writers give up writing, simply because they feel their efforts have not justified their years of labour. A sort of public indifference throws them into silence. This is because they write on the assumption that whatever they have created should be read, or else writing would not have served its purpose. There are many who fall into this category, lapsing into a silence of their own making, when they find that all they have written has not been able to *touch* a single reader. The consequence is that they cease to write, the passion of their youth gone, their need gone; having come to the conclusion that the painful struggle of writing had failed them, other things in life taking up the place of writing those writers had zealously upheld so far.

It is also true that one may come across writers who do not have the need to publish, without losing their need to write. Uncommon though this is, we have examples in the life of Emily Dickinson, the American poet, whose work was only published after her lifetime. I know of at least one Indian poet who has written some very powerful and committed verse in our country but has chosen not to publish a book. There may be others who continue to write on in the privacy of their own homes, but without having the need to publish, even in a small publication or magazine. The poet chooses to live in a silent world of his own making, not wanting to share his creations. The significance of this sort of silence is perhaps understood more by the poet himself than by other practising friend-poets; for such a silence is a fusion of understanding and indulgence, when the intelligence seems to transcend itself, attaining such heights that are above the thinking domain of a normal person. To such a poet who uses his silence as a part of living, it helps to discover and consecrate the events of his life, a life which makes him truly vulnerable to the usual passions of a writer, airs and conceit among them.

Emily Dickinson was one who did not lose her sense of time, as most of us do; her silence was to her the consequence of the natural act of writing poetry. It doesn't matter to us today that she was not there when her poetry was published, as it didn't matter to her. We have the inheritance of her poetry; and as with all poets who are dead, these dead continue to nourish the living. But the fact that a poet herself chose silence to sustain the poetry she wrote in her lifetime, gives us a new perspective on the purpose she carried—the desire in making something impersonal of her poetry.

Because of such an impersonality, the work, to all accounts, leads to perfection. One is tempted to think of those numerous nameless craftsmen, artists and builders who went on to create many of the most marvellous works of art through the ages, and which are a continuing source of delight. These *perfect* examples of artistic excellence were made by artists, who worked wholly to create, were unconcerned about leaving their signatures for posterity. The superb temples of South and Southwest Asia and the medieval cathedrals of Europe are evidence enough of the creations of the impersonal artist. Their facelessness, their silence goes deep into our hearts to heighten our understanding of the way our own lives shape under the realities of existence.

But what exactly is it that brings a writer to a state of silence? It is best to leave aside the justification that indifference or cataclysmic events torment him so much as to trigger off the idea of futility of writing; and we might better set aside the thought that the poet's heart reaches that condition when poetry appears to him in all its nakedness until he finally decides to purge his soul of the falseness of words. The French poet, Paul Valery, in his celebrated play, *Dance and the Soul,* said that "Life blackens at the contact of truth, as a suspicious mushroom blackens when it is crushed, at the contact of the air." One is drawn to ask: Does some such thing happen in the case of a serious writer, when he decides that his life's work has reached that moment of truth? Or is it the last touch to a masterpiece of delirious power?

It is hard to answer these. I can only confirm that one is faced, at one time or other, with the substance of silence. It is a silence which seems to save, to redeem. And this silence is no magician's trick. It is not even the shriek of a man falling out of a high window. Nor the sound before an ocean wave breaks. Or a wound which refuses to heal.

One must agree though, that only through words will one ever be able to find that silence. A silence which is simply what it means, nothing else. No poetic symbol or prophetic order. *Just that word.*

But to achieve that silence, a poet has to test every word and emotion to the breaking point. I may not be right in saying this, because writing itself has always been a difficult act for me. Perhaps Eliot's remark about emotion and personality seems totally convincing: "only those who have personality and emotions know what it means to want to escape from those things." Janos Pilinszky, that distinguished Hungarian poet whose recent work moves positively toward that search for truth, has shown in poems like "Green" a mysterious clue of silence:

> My eyes sink, my face, my soul,
> every living being immersed
> in that bottomless green
> which is a tree within, without.
>
> (Trs. Peter Jay)

The Japanese haiku, pared down to essentials, seems to hold that extraordinary sensation of silence. Reading a poet like Basho, one feels that his poetry is able to conquer silence as nobody's else's; he just doesn't stand on ceremony with it. His poems cherish it, as silence seems to watch over our destiny:

> An old pond:
> A frog jumps in—
> The sound of water.

Life teaches us much. Yet a lot of life remains uncovered. The fundamental question of why life began; and if it began, why it is going to die, is what we are finally left with. For it is quite evident that death too, like life itself, will not tell us anything we really want to know.

And if writing creatively, be it prose or poetry, or whatever, becomes a useless gesture in the end, without having served any purpose, one faces the wall the writer knows he will have to risk sometime. The writing of his entire lifetime, then, does not appear even symbolic to him. But this is how I feel, as I realise it might not be generally applicable.

When we consider a poem by Juan Ramon Jimenez, for example:

> Time, give me the secret
> that makes you younger as
> you grow older!
>
> Day after day, your past
> falls away, and your future looms ahead,
> —and your present:
> always the same as the instant
> of the almond blossoming!
>
> Time without footprints:
> tell me how your soul
> daily flows through your body!

I feel that one is experiencing here the essence of things. Let us forget what the poem is trying to say. What the poem is about. I care because of the poem's touch, because this touch is a feeling that the poet's own longing has brought me. And the poet imparts to his readers and listeners this touch of beauty, keeping for himself only his longing that he needs to make his poems. So, this pursuit this impact of beauty, is a small push toward silence.

And I would say we are only faced with a silence which words have brought us ultimately to; all the words we thought were grand exercises of imagination, fusing the imaginary with reality. This silence is not just a stock character of mystery, or a knowledge, a knowledge that is always provisional. Nor is it some kind of wound that one would wait for it to heal.

Maybe we owe words this silence we need in the end. For after the words have been said, one asks: Will poetry continue to exile us from life by words we no longer have the right to share? Or is it that we will only know how to use words, when, as in the Book of Job, 13: 13, Job says:

> Let me have silence, and I will speak...?

30

On the Mountain with Allen Ginsberg

"Lovely blue shirt....Moustache!"

"Yes," I answered, "an Indian brand." "Blue," he mused, more to himself than to anyone else, immersed in his own thoughts.

He looks up, his eyes intense, deep and penetrating. Perhaps the eyes of a child, I think, a child's eyes looking on something new, as though for the first time. His gaze fans the tall pines along the Colorado mountain slopes, and rests on a snow sheet partly covering the mountain side.

"I bought it in India," I said, to keep the conversation going, I suppose. The denim shirt I wore quivered a little in the cool wind. We walked slowly, carefully up the rocky path, Allen following a few steps behind, as breathless as I was in the thin Rocky Mountain air.

Allen Ginsberg looks frail. There seems to be an unmistakable shuffle in his walk as he puts each step slowly forward. Fiercely independent, he moves on, denying help. I wait for him to catch up with me.

"How old are you?" he asks.

"Sixty-five."

"You are in pretty good shape," he comments. A little weak today, his spirit is undefeated. He is just a few years older to me.

It was the thirteenth of July and I had finished reading my poetry the evening before at Boulder's Performing Arts Center. It had been an exciting event, although somewhat bizarre, this reading I had shared with three young American poets; and I had requested the people at the Naropa Institute to take me up the mountains that rose sharply from the city limits of Boulder.

But I appeared to reel still from the shock I got at the reading of the evening before, when a young and pretty African-American poet called Akilah Oliver took off her shirt when she started to read, right there in front of everyone on the podium. This was something I had never expected. And then Akilah had gone on to remove her bra, her gestures casual, her face expressionless. I gulped. Sitting in the front row, I stole a glance at Allen and Anne Waldman and Lorenzo Thomas seated alongside. The world had not changed. And then I heard Akilah's nonchalant announcement: "You may take your clothes off if you wish." She began reading. The spot played on her bare shoulders.

Michael and Josh were the two youngsters who had gladly agreed to drive us into the mountains. They were strong and athletic, full of the enthusiasm that makes youth take those leaps across the garden fence we older men can only admire. I watched Allen attentively for some time as he rested for a while on the grassy knoll spread out at the foot of the snow sheet. The weak murmur of melting snow reached our ears. Rills of water left the grained whiteness to flow down somewhere below us.

A strange sound cut into the silence. I looked around me. I could see nothing anywhere. Suddenly the tops of the pines to the far left began to sway. It was the wind, sweeping through the trees in a wide arc. The sound floated in, confident, wise; further proof of a knowledge patterned by centuries of earth and sky.

Maybe the blue of denims made Allen nostalgic for the youth he had lost. The blue. Like the clear blue of the sky above I saw him staring into.

Lithe and quick, Michael had already moved away from us and was trying to run up the precarious snow sheet. His voice carried loud and clear in the wind. "Look," he shouted, "we're getting into trouble!"

Josh was close by. The two of them had run up to the top of the slope and were trying to slide down, using the soles of their shoes as leverage on the snow. Allen had become wistful all of a sudden. The distant look in his eyes seemed to flash over my thoughts.

"The young. Nothing concerns them."

He turned to me. "Such a change to see the boys getting into trouble." I didn't know what to answer. Youth was way behind us, but it was obvious that Allen was more than simply nostalgic. Maybe it was hard for him to accept the sadness that comes with age. There was regret in his gaze, much of it, his rainbows had become black and white, and his trees were bone. And my fears were strengthened when he began to recite some stanzas from a poem, about youth lost, about the weight of age.

It was a lost poem.

Or maybe there was the fear of the unknown in his eyes, I cannot say. We were now stretched out on the grass, each immersed in his own thoughts. The sun's warmth dug into our bodies. The two boys had disappeared over the rise some time back with the warning that they would be back in an hour after they had done a bit of climbing.

Allen began reading some parts of my "Orissa Journal", a prose piece I had written for the *Hudson Review* in recent years. "I like this," he said, looking up, "when you speak of the different levels of time that can adhere to a single instant." I wanted to tell him that time, as we knew and understood it in India, was never linear. "It's cyclic," I put in. "It does not end like when you switch off a lamp in a room. In Orissa, when you are witnessing an event like the Ratha Jatra festival in Puri, you are simply part of a totality. The mythical, the historic and the present are all united and one. That's what makes life very different there from that in the West."

He nodded. He put the essay away. He started singing softly to himself the first two lines of an Indian hymn we all loved. Gandhiji's favourite hymn.

Raghupati Raghava Raja Ram
Patita Pavana Sita Ram...

He went on singing. Love for things Indian perhaps, I reasoned. Or love for India itself. Or because his Indian adventure in the early sixties had not ended once it had begun, it is difficult to say.

Allen Ginsberg had become an acknowledged Buddhist. But here he was, seated on a high mountain slope, singing Hindu bhajans. I wasn't trying to understand him. He started showing me the postures of meditation he practised, the legs crossed, the hands stretched forward, palms turned toward the sky. It was a ritual at Naropa.

"To receive," he explained, pointing at his palms turned upward. I demonstrated to him the Buddhist *asana* I knew, where the thumb is almost folded into the palm. "This is the Tibetan way," he went on, going into the modes he knew.

A little later, Allen and I climbed up the slope above us. It was tough going. We paused at intervals, taking in the vista around us. Away in the distance lay the city of Boulder, which we had left four hours before.

The boys hadn't returned. I heard Allen shout out loud, "Michael! Josh!" The mountains distorted his calls. No answer came.

We descended slowly. Allen seemed light-headed. He began to narrate the incident at Puri thirty years ago when he had forced his way into the temple of Lord Jagannath.

"How did you manage it?" I prodded him.

I remember having heard about this incident earlier from Anne Waldman, poet and Program Director at Naropa. Apparently Allen never got tired talking about it; a strong feeling of pride was always evident in his recounting of the tale.

"I took a chance and decided to enter the temple," he said. I suppose Allen's skin had probably lost its fairness after his wanderings across India. He went on, "And there I was in the courtyard which was totally banned to those who were not Hindus. It was fascinating." His eyes lighted up. "Then a priest suddenly found out I was a Westerner. I didn't know what to do. I let myself go. I lay prostrate in front of him, at the priest's feet. I folded my hands. I begged. Then another priest came along. I did the same thing again. I lay down at his feet and begged forgiveness. And there was another one. But I got through," he finished, success showing in his eyes.

I was taken aback. Even the late Prime Minister of India, Indira Gandhi, was denied admission into the temple. "Can I quote you?" I asked Allen. He said, "Yes, certainly," and turned to the boys again.

We were in the car back to Boulder. Allen had hardly an hour before his lecture to students at the Summer Writing Program at Naropa. Still he seemed quite relaxed. He began chanting the lines of the old hymn again as we drove downhill.

I didn't know what to do. I joined in.

31

Containing the World that Contains Us: Myth/Symbol as Metaphor in Poetry

As I begin this piece, or for that matter, any statement or essay, the first question which comes to my mind is: Am I sincere? Am I honest? Am I going to be absolutely truthful to myself in what I am about to say?

This simple question raises enough doubts in my mind. It is easier, plainer to talk about another person's sincerity; let's say, when someone important makes a statement to praise a soap or fabric in a television commercial—but this much is true, that it becomes difficult to tell when I myself am sincere. The question comes back to me because I would be asking myself next: That if *I* am unsure about my own honesty, how can I speak so surely of another's?

One can possibly extend this to the example of a poem, because here I should like to restrict myself primarily to the subject of poetry. When one writes a poem, probably the outcome of the poem would depend on how honest he or she is—and by outcome, I would mean the measure by which the intensities of the poem have been communicated to the reader. To a great extent, I feel, the poet's sincerity would contribute to the poem's feel.

I might also like to speak here of the poem itself and of the poet in relation to the poem. By the very act of writing the poem, the poet is learning to feel himself. When I am reading someone else's writing, then my own response to the work may be, broadly speaking, of two kinds—original and fresh and sincere; or, derivative, cliched and insincere. Probably my reaction, my conviction to the poem's sincerity would build from the thought or the ideas of the poem, which the poet finds out *not* through spontaneity or what we might call inspiration (a terrible enough word)—but through a process of careful thinking, which means again a scrupulous and exact weighing of the words the poet makes before they are finally incorporated into the poem.

And so, the poet learns how to feel by writing the poem.

And, in the writing of the poem, when the poet takes language and idea and a sense of music and welds these together to form a certain unity (which we can term a poem), it is the poet's imagination which *becomes* the movement that makes the poem. This imagination acts basically in two ways: (1) when the movement is from image to image, it is used concretely and (2) when the movement is from thought to thought, it moves abstractly.

It is difficult for me to speak about these two divisions in the imagination, simply because I have myself utilised both these concepts in my own work—and I cannot exactly say why I have done these things the way they appear in my poems, and how. It is just that I am considering here a matter of the imagination, which comes through because of my own approach and enthusiasm.

Working the imagination, to my mind, represents the beating of the heart in the poem. And such working is effected by metaphor, which is, bluntly speaking, *vision*. It is this metaphor we are merely talking about, for poetry can intimidate or astonish the reader through the use of metaphor.

Robert Frost once said: "I do not think anybody ever knows the discreet use of metaphor, his own and other people's, the discreet handling of metaphor, unless he has been properly educated in poetry." In plainer words, we could say that if one learns anything through poetry, it is the same as learning through metaphor.

Poetry travels through metaphors. These metaphors may be trivial and commonplace at one end, be beautiful too, and may also go on to be very profound and deep tropes at the other extreme. As I said, metaphors provide vision in some way or other, thereby adding another dimension to the substance of poetry. And perhaps through the medium of poetry (or, through metaphorical use), we could say something and mean another. This is expressly what has happened in some of my own poems. I should like to give an example of these different ways of thinking which can happen in a poem I wrote years ago, titled "Indian Summer":

> Over the soughing of the summer wind,
> priests chant louder than ever:
> the mouth of India opens.
> Crocodiles move into deeper waters
> ....

I have, here, quoted the first part of the poem as that would be adequate for our needs.

Now, to the poem, which speaks of summer months in India, especially in Orissa where I have lived all my life, and which is a hard, trying period for most people. And, I suppose, because people spend sleepless days and nights due to the excessive heat, more rituals and festivals have been accommodated into these hot and sultry days. So, traditionally, the temple, which represents the hub of village and town life, is astir with movement and activity—keeping priests busier than before.

I shall not try to clarify here what *I* have done in the poem, but should only like to point at different areas of thinking, which could have been mine or not. When I referred to "the mouth of India" and said that it "opens", the statement could literally deal with the hunger of our people, spiritual of course (the physical one being always there, and cannot be denied even today), and which opens in the manner of a fledgling opening its mouth. But this one is the more apparent meaning. A poet would always like to talk in parables and speculative words. And it is here that a deep-rooted Hindu myth comes into being, with the idea or picture of Krishna opening his mouth on the battlefield of Kurukshetra and revealing the ultimate reality to Arjuna. Possibly every Indian has come into contact with the *Mahabharata* and the *Bhagavad Gita*, and can very well connect this "mouth of India" in the poem with Krishna's revelation without effort from his or her side.

In this use of "the mouth of India", the metaphor is *a form of expansion*—where, the mind, in its mysterious working, has gone on to add one thing to another. One could call this an audacious metaphor—something which came suddenly to my mind then—but such a leaping metaphor becomes, undoubtedly, the life-blood of the poem. To a Western reader of the poem, this mythical image would certainly be unknown; instead, maybe, the metaphor would communicate something else to his mind—indeed, something as significant. Or else, how would I explain the first publication of this poem in a periodical of such significance as the *Times Literary Supplement?*

The mind is a monstrous computer, which can excel in linking things in many different ways. When I look at a blob of spilled ink on a sheet of paper, it reminds me of various things: it becomes the shadow on a wall I noticed once on a dark evening in my childhood, it becomes the solitude of the sea on a moonless night. It is really amazing how one thing leads straightaway to another, how these leaps occur in the imagination without conscious effort of any kind. And unconscious thought becomes the substance of the poem—in many of the poems I have written—this thought, which moves out of me, growing into the poem. It is as though my mind reaches everywhere, and as I go on facing my own experiences in my life, my thought is responsible for becoming those metaphors that ultimately contain my poetry.

I have already said that not all metaphors bring forth good poetry; some are trite, and weaken the poem. I realise sadly too, that at times, I am guilty of producing puerile, cliched poems. An instance comes to my mind, of the *lakshman-rekha,* the mythical circle which Lakshman marked on the ground for Sita not to step outside of it. The metaphoric use of the circle in Indian literary history cannot be denied; it represents a part of our living, and has strong moral overtones for the reader. In my long poem, *Temple*, I have used the concept of the *lakshman-rekha* as a measure of the life Chelammal (the protagonist) has to come to terms with perhaps to fight with her death. My point here is to stress, that I have, once again, used this myth as metaphor (a cliche surely), although the suitability of such an use can become a matter for argument.

Often the human mind can take wild, awesome leaps into the unconscious, and come out with metaphors of dizzying dimensions. Here is the dream-mind's unbelievable ability to create its own beings. And while these "beings" the mind invents can be totally disparate objects, it is the metaphor which finds out their likenesses, linking one to the other, although they may be widely separated by space and time. Perhaps, in the character of Chelammal in *Temple,* in this very ordinary woman, can come to life the mind and body of Putana, and this life of mythical evil Chelammal has unconsciously inherited from her former self—to cope with her life.

With the complexity of behaviour seen around us, such as a mechanical device, an electrical circuit, a wildlife migration, a rioting crowd, an atmospheric storm, or a national economy—it seems only plausible that these are governed by a multitude of independent factors or subject to random influences. Physicists look for complex causes in complex results. And the only way they could see a solution was to assert that chaos was an integral part in nature. So, if disorder is a reality in nature, would it be unwise to expect disorderly jumps in the making of a poem?

Even with my basic training in Physics, I am at times awed by some metaphors that are widely used. Higher physics and mathematics have given us a metaphor that still sounds unthinkable: the relationship between mass and energy, and which Einstein translated so aptly into the equation $E=mc^2$. How can the mind conceive that a tiny speck of matter is equivalent to an enormous amount of energy? Or another which states that the tree I saw standing outside the window a second ago was not exactly there when I looked at it? It is difficult to comprehend this too, because the fact of observation itself is uncertain, linked as it is with the passage of time and with the fact that we are always moving.

A metaphor which fancifully caught me when I was working on *Relationship*, and later on went into *Temple* again, was what I termed "the sleep-habit of the golden deer". Maybe this metaphor was inappropriate, but that again is another matter. However, to my mind, this metaphor represented the liberating character of the poem, perhaps the poem's life-blood. "Sleep" as a symbol, as an experience I have perhaps sought all my life, of that sense of order that emerges from desire—and which the dream-mind in me craved for:

> This sleep is a song
> that is heard from all sides continually,
> a coarse cage that can hold a larger life,
> a time that stretches the scarlet in the mind

> and graces the heart's skies with clear wind,
> the hiding-place without beginning or end,
> and the largest circle that transcends
> the angles of man's consciousness,
> a blind eye that creates the special vision
> of our poignant significance.
>
> (*Relationship*, Sec.V)

In the above passage, I have gone into the metaphor of "sleep", believing what I wrote, in sincerity and complete honesty, and not with the cleverness that readers and critics attribute sometimes to the poetry. To my mind, "sleep" moves on to the idea of a "cage", and then expands to "the largest circle" that exists beyond man's consciousness. I suppose the metaphor of sleep has taken leaps into the unconscious, producing its own train of thought. And each of these "likenesses" or metaphors adds up somehow to a kind of harmonic symmetry that thought produces, without compromising much logic in the poem.

It should be apparent from these examples (I have deliberately chosen from my own work) how to a great extent the sensibility is haunted by metaphors linked to myth and symbol.

Whitman has done wonderfully bold and ambitious things in his "Song of Myself", taking "grass" and likening it to the "handkerchief of the Lord". Finally, one is amazed and one experiences a sense of acceptance when he says:

> Or I guess the grass itself is a child,
> the produced babe of the vegetation.

Even a simple symbol such as "rain" has gone on to induce diverse meanings in my own poems, and it is true that the mind or brain finds such new shapes and resemblances through a kind of biological urging I find hard to explain. I cannot also oppose the fact that the process of metaphoric use brings a consciousness in poetry that turns into masses of words and phrases, as though they were shells rising to the surface, shells bright and strange, and resonant with the accumulated echoes of their past histories. For these are what move the mind, with their drama and their power. And doing just this, with sincerity, gives one much pleasure, artistically; as one draws experience out of memory, building metaphor, seeking the lightness of living that is perhaps poetry.

32

The SAARC Writers: Suffering from Our Poetry

The Hungarian composer, Bela Bartok, once wrote in a letter to a friend: "I have lost confidence in people, in countries, in everything." This was in 1941, when the Second World War was at its height. Today, sixty years after he said this, the truth of his words cannot be denied. I suppose one cannot be both tragic and human at the same time, especially at times of crises such as war or revolution or terrorism; and each is an event of the utmost misfortune for us. These are moments when the illogical becomes logical, and a victory turns to loss. Our countries in this region are the victims of terrible acts, imprisonments, killings and burnings. One doesn't even know how many undiscovered graves there are around us. It is difficult for a writer to foresee the ultimate aim of these things. Can I forget, as an Indian, living amidst so-called civilised human beings, the cruel and savage act of the burning to death of a missionary and his two young children simply because they belonged to another faith? Any sensitive person would not be able to put aside the thought of the agony and the cries of the two children on that cold January night! And a poet is supposed to be a sensitive, feeling person, probably more than the man who delivers your morning paper or your milk. And so the poet will write about what he sees—and what we might call as poetry of witness—in his longing for truth through his own manner of direction and his innocence.

A long time back I read Laxmi Prasad Devkota's poem titled "Make Me a Sheep, O God!" in an English translation.

The Nepali poet's commonplace words still keep ringing in my ears:

> Let me not jump to the void like a sage.
> Or with an artificial imagination.
> Let me not create distorted magic of variegated colours out of magicless truth.
> Let me not become a Brahmin to live on dirty water washing away others' sin.
> ...
> Let me not reform to expose the world.
> Let me not patch up the old and tattered things.
> Let me lit the light of life,
> Like the simple, beautiful, and unbeautiful light of Nature,
> When dying
> Let me reach higher up than the sage...

Perhaps art or literature or the word is seen by this Nepali poet (and other poets of this region whom I've read in English translation) as a moving, unsettling experience. This is something that appears to challenge the writer's and reader's vision of our world:

> Say it, don't be afraid,
> Against the tyranny
> which doesn't allow us to hold our heads high,
> Against the poetry which does not allow us to speak,
> Against the poetry which does not allow us to live,
> Against the ignorance which allows us to know nothing...

Such lines by another Nepali poet, Gopal Prasad Rimal, depend on bare-bone simplicity. Many will find fault with such writing, written in conditions of extremity, and which rely on the immediacies of direct address. But this is an intimate, naked sort of poetry—a poetry in which lurk signs of hope, and which has been practised by the great poets of Eastern Europe and Latin America. Like these poets, some of our poets live inside history, the history of their respective countries, and under the lingering, overall shadow of colonisation. Therefore it would be right to insist that their imaginations are enlivened by that very perspective.

It is well known that atrocities have happened, and are still taking place on an unprecedented scale in the countries of this region for the last many years. Such monstrous acts have come to be regarded as almost normal. One has only to open the morning newspaper to find evidences of these acts. And it becomes easier to forget than to remember, and this forgetfulness becomes our defence against remembering. Perhaps a reader would tend to reject such a poem as one filled with unnecessary sentimentality. Earlier, I referred to a cruel incident in my own state of Orissa. So if I write a poem about this, or about a recent starvation death in Orissa, would it only be a futile exercise in sentimentality?

For instance, when Al Mahmud writes such a poem from his native Bangladesh, do we dismiss it as just another sentimental narrative? I'd like to quote from his "Wing-breaking":

> I cry as those birds cry, rising like black flags crying aloud...
> ...
> Why do such sounds of weeping arise today? Until now,
> tortoises of the Bastami pool's turbid water
> were the pattern of living; who, hoping for long, easy life,
> used to catch and seize thrown-away food.
> Crimson meat-pulp-like, greed would come spattering
> and falling slimily everyday on the landing steps.
> ...
> In the whole country's deep roar
> the sound of my name has surrounded my body
> and like cricket-swilling pervaded the village.

And, in another poem, he says, thinking of Van Gogh:

> Rats run away leaving in the poet's notebook
> the severed ear of the artist.
> And like a near-blind poet,
> groping for my tobacco pouch,
> I pick up the just-cut ear of Van Gogh.

Is this mere sentimentality? I wouldn't say so. Al Mahmud's feeling-lines come from, and are a record, of experience—his own. Consequently, the poem becomes an exhortation and a plea against despair.

One could go on to cite such examples of poetry written in other SAARC countries; poems that are not merely cries for sympathy but are a call for strength. We speak about our visions and our aspirations in the new century we find ourselves in today, but these visions will only depend on what our societies and countries do for us. The history of our time does not allow for any anaesthetic of progress. Perhaps we can only retell this history in the fragmentary images of our time. Like contemporary poets elsewhere (James Fenton, the British poet, in "Lines for Translation into Any Language" offers the same bleak analysis: the story of war, or life in and around a cemetery) our poetry too will only go on to reflect the darkness of this vision.

Therefore one can understand when the Sri Lankan poet, Siri Gunasinghe, speaks of "a long journey,/ a grief-filled journey." And that journey progresses "from darkness to darkness." Every poet writing seriously in our region will build his or her poem on the resistance to false attempts at justice by people and by governments everywhere. What other ideal can a writer have? His poetry may take different forms; it can be impassioned or ironic. It can speak in the language of the common man or in an esoteric language that is not easily understood. But the poet wants to be heard. He wants the world to know him, in the way he lives and dies. He writes with a view; a view that the planet in which we live remains a place fit for human habitation. And his recklessness shows, like that of Iftikhar Arif of Pakistan, when he writes:

> All armies are the same, all swords are the same.
> Light mowed down by hooves of horses.
> ...
> It's always the same.
> And every time the aftermath—a realm of total silence.
> A silence that swallows
> the terror and horror of victorious drumming.

How very true these lines sound today! The protest of these writers against violence will not be easily forgotten. We need to remember, as we go on hearing their words—and realise that poetry is always more than what words can say. Kedarnath Singh, the Hindi poet, wrote in one of his poems: "I am in the place/where things no longer exist." Like him, I too feel unsure where I am; and whether I am on my way to paradise or to the heart of darkness doesn't matter much to me.

33

The Absence of Absolutes

I should like to suppose that the main part of a poet's work (or any artist's, for that matter) is not the creation itself so much as invocation. This appears to be especially relevant for poetry written in India. The significance of our strong oral tradition cannot be underrated. And an invocation or worship seemed but a normal defence for a universal integrity. We can take, for instance, Gangadhar Meher's poetry in Oriya.

When one writes, one is just not aware that he is making it, this poem, or creating it; but that this part of his creation must be received. How does one receive, or get this gift except, perhaps, by supplication? In other words, does he receive it by creating within himself this "begging bowl" to which the gift is drawn? It would not be wrong to assume that there are few artists who have not had this sense that some element in their work comes to them from a source they do not control. Maybe something really happens to a poet (I speak for myself) when he has written a good poem. At such a moment I feel both empty and full, I like to be alone at first, and yet not entirely alone, but with that living invisible Presence that is there inside of me. And I would like to run to the bank of the secluded river where I spent the early years of my life, and hold the silent cry of the sky and of the water pressed to my heart. If there are tears in the eyes then, it is some meaningful form, a form that love might take, or annihilation or death. And maybe I feel I am being pulled under the warm waters of the Kathjodi where I grew up.

Allen Ginsberg has talked about this gift in relation to the poet's creation. The gift will come to you only when "it means abandoning being a poet, abandoning your careerism, abandoning even the idea of writing any poetry, really abandoning, giving up as hopeless—abandoning the possibility of really expressing yourself to the world. Abandoning the idea of being a prophet with honour and dignity, and abandoning the glory of poetry and just settling down in the muck of your own mind.... You really have to make a resolution just to write for yourself...in the sense of not writing to impress yourself, but just writing what your self is saying."

To approach words for a poem is more an act of worship. I suppose a poet (I am speaking of us, as writers of our country) goes about this in the manner of a ritual, invocating a magic he feels is there in the language he'd use.

The very use of a word, and the associations with other words, pushes the poet into the darkened mind-room where the poet invariably collides with the phantoms of words enveloped in their familiar old shrouds. The unexplored darkness of the room urges him on; in actuality the poet doesn't know what awaits him in the dark. There is this sensuality of his which is the prime mover of the writing of the poem; and his intelligence, which I am afraid to say, at times, instead of helping him to get along, stands in the way of the total effectiveness of the poem.

My sensuality broke through early in my life, this I can truthfully admit. But the sudden sense of what life was offering to me lay amidst confusion and ignorance. The outside world took over without my knowing. I began pulling at both light and shadow. The waves of affection and solitude set me adrift. I was twelve. And I suddenly realised my true nature was romantic.

There was nothing much to do, but my main purpose to study. As a boy I did well in Science and in Mathematics, although my interests appeared to be elsewhere—in books of the imagination, the romantic novels of Walter Scott and H. Rider Haggard. And R.M. Ballantyne. The reading of these books made me surrender myself to a world far removed from my own, one that held a kind of melancholy in harmony with the haughtiness of heroics the characters in the books provided.

Or, perhaps, was it a time of the beginning of my love for myself?

It is difficult to answer such questions. Like the impulse that made me sit down to write. Of course this struggle to write came in later, when I was twenty-two, and had mastered (or so I thought) the language which I would use. English came naturally to me, a consequence of my schooling in a missionary school in Cuttack, then run by a British couple. It would not be incorrect to state that my British headmaster was responsible for inculcating in me a strong love for the English language. In those days we weren't even allowed to speak any other language except English in school; our library, with its many books, was always ready to set me moving with long silences with myself. I was alone, but had begun to cut my way out to a new freedom.

No one asked then, all those formative years, as to why I was reading English. The language never ceased to fascinate me, but I wouldn't like to speak of that now. I loved to play with those alien words, turning the words around, waiting for the effect these changes would bring. But I hadn't given a thought to writing then, except for the few imaginative exercises we did in our language class in school. I read too about the many colonies of Britain, and of the vastness of the British Empire—all these were taught as part of our Geography course in the Junior and Senior Cambridge classes. But I never thought of myself that I was colonised. And was a victim of some sort in this set-up, as some thought.

An ingrained sadness never left me, I think. It hasn't still. A child is dwarfed by his parents, uncles and aunts. And as a student, by his school. As the youngest boy in my class, as one who came from a lower middle-class background, the indignities I suffered from my classmates pushed me into a corner. Books became my safe haven. I realised I could stay alone, only by seeking refuge in the world of books and escape being victimised by the bullying seniors in my class.

I mention all this briefly to relate a little of the background that perhaps impelled me to write. I don't remember how my writing exactly came into being; I was always restless and weak, always feeling I had more than my share of sorrow in this world, and life in the home, after school, was no less painful to me.

It seemed natural to me that I would shy away from the ostentatious community of human relationships.

Today my concern is the written word. The word that speaks of the human condition. For the human spirit is what seems to matter, no less for us in India. It would not be far from wrong if one suggested that our way of life is a way of art. The art of living is founded on rhythm, on giving and receiving, ebb and flow, darkness and light, life and death. For years we have had our reasons to believe in the view that life is not linear, but has to be lived in a cycle. Maybe this is what differentiates the Indian from the Western idea of living. And this is what comes to be in one's writing, mine.

When I started writing poetry in the late sixties, I never thought of these issues. The writing of a poem, of bringing a particular feeling to form, and choosing the words for the poem seemed to be all. My feelings then, I suppose, were quite simple. One took up, simply speaking, an experience, and went on to assimilate it in a poem. With no knowledge of poetry behind me, and with a background of physics, I believed writing could be fulfilled through discipline, just as in the case of science. Here maybe I was wrong. But my poetry rested, as with others of my tribe, on a seemingly religious view of life; and this meant the positive acceptance of pain, suffering, defeat and misfortune that came one's way. I began to write in the manner I experienced living; feeling the wrong, the lie, the nastiness and the injustice I perceived around me; and could go on to question the existence of God whom my parents had taught me scrupulously to believe in.

Because English came to me naturally enough, I wrote my beginning poems in English—not in Oriya, my mother tongue. I did not realise then that a poem could be of interest or significance to certain people and totally devoid of meaning or charm to others. But I wrote on. I wrote about what I saw, felt, or perceived. Maybe that was enough for me. When my first book of poetry was reviewed way back in 1972, an already established poet-reviewer, speaking about the book, labelled me "a poem maker". In other words, the reviewer said I was not writing "poetry". I asked myself then, over and over again, if what he had said was correct. And I thought he was. I thought there was a furious discipline in the use of my words, but it was true that the feeling was lost in the words of the poems. And I had to bring my feeling out from the edifice of life that I called the poem—in the poetry I would write next. This did not seem easy. I thought only of myself, not of anything else. I was not participating in the affairs of the community. Nor was I a dedicated man of science as was my vocation, or was I deep into any philosophical thought. Only there was a strange agony in me I couldn't put aside. Age, which was creeping in on me, was an imaginary monster that kept tormenting my days. The rawness of the world made me writhe. And I was trying to discover new postures, turning myself inside out, to protect myself with the words of my poems.

As a boy in school I was introduced to the bizarre world of Alice. Frankly, I'd like to admit I could not understand then what her "wonderland" was. Today when I pick up the same lines of Lewis Carroll I'd read when I was young, I feel they mean much more than the blank glitter the words then revealed. "When I use a word," Humpty Dumpty said in a rather scornful tone, "it means just what I chose it to mean—neither more nor less." The profound significance of this statement hits me today, more because of the use of words in my poems. And yet I appear to ask: Can this be truthfully applied to in the case of poetry? It is the moment that decides on the exact sense of a word; for when I write the word "love" today, isn't its meaning quite different from my understanding of that word when I was eighteen?

But I suppose one has to go on writing what one has to write. Slowly there emerged from my life an intriguing, melancholy poetry. I insist on the word "intriguing" because of an inherent egoism I now believe had shaped my poems—that must have come from my basic science training coupled with the stupid indulgence of mine that made me feel I could excel in poetry just in the manner I had done well in physics. And yet I remained all the time discontented with my efforts to write poetry.

Maybe this discontent helped me to write. I kept on with my efforts at observation of the things around me, which I thought was one of the main prerequisites of a poet; and a seemingly purposeless observation filled me with the purpose of writing poetry. There were times when I went through extremes of experience, and it was but a natural consequence of these periods when I found that the language of the poem did not conform to the set standards of syntax or form. Consciousness then, at such times, doesn't remain whole; it is crucified on the cross of language. When life exposes one's most private, once miraculous, sacred body on the sacrificial slab, draining away blood and suffering and despair, poetry is relegated towards the speech of speechlessness, finding itself in the passion of reintegrating into some mysterious form or essence. One could term this limiting node to be a sort of dead silence of the poem, where the unspeakable springs up like a violent hot spring and carries the language out of the poem.

However, it was hard to understand the disapproval and the antipathy one experienced because of the use of English in one's poetry. When I began writing I was oblivious to this opposition, which was directed mostly from academics in colleges and universities, who taught English and American literature and were poets themselves, writing in their own regional languages. Later, after I had published a few collections, their pointed barbs did hurt me. It became obvious I was an outsider, merely because I was writing in English. (I am afraid my literary friends still treat me in that manner today, especially in Orissa, although I have published four collections of Oriya poetry in the past decade. There could be reasons for this unacceptability of course, and they might well be of a personal nature.) Nevertheless it became apparent that the world grew appreciably smaller because I was fairly successful in writing poetry in English. To understand the criminality of language, I told myself, was not my concern. Whether English as a language was the accomplice of colonials did not matter. My intentions were honourable, and that was all.

Poetry is where the language happens. In poetry, as in nowhere else, language gets examined for the truths it contains. Maybe the words keep dying and always coming back to life. The world of the mind is made of language. It is the foetus in which people see and think, because it is the foetus that gives way to birth of the feeling for life through a sieve of words. Plainly speaking, the world comes to us through words and is expressed by us in words. So poetry is a sort of surrender to the flux of language, a language born out of both history and society. This implies that poems are where the language gets made; made because of the belief the poet has in himself or herself, in his role or mission. And through poetry language either gets richer or poorer, healthier or sicker. Poetry has no choice. When language fails, poetry fails too.

To get to the fundamentals, poetry does not make things happen. That is what language does. Poetry is about making language happen. It is we who push our language to do things in all spheres of our lives.

Until recent times, when I looked at the poems I had written, I couldn't see the burden on the language of the poems, on the language's tolerance and its provocation. That there is this powerful purpose of reaching out in the language, that it was always on the edge of touching someone, that it was communal. Each one of us practises his craft in solitude, in the privacy of our rooms, but we tend to overlook the fact that the words of the language we use have been spoken or read or written any number of times by numbers of people—even though we try to manipulate those same words in poetry. And on those words the lives of others rest.

Therefore, those poems of mine that appeared in print then, and some which I still write today, sound obscure to the few who read and discuss them. Einsteinian physics postulates that the behaviour of things is dependent on the position and state of their viewer. Does this hold for poetry too? I am referring here to reviewers and readers who felt earlier my poetry was and that it still is opaque. It would not be of much use to anyone if I explained that those very poems are transparent to me. Maybe I didn't understand my own self. Or perhaps I was ignorant about the language I used in my poems and about the lives of others through which language passed on its way to me.

Today, years of living and writing seem to have changed my attitude towards poetry and life. The act of writing poetry is essentially one of faith; it is the despair I feel, the upheaval of values in me that I want the reader to feel. I remember a line of Proust which says: "Man is the creature who cannot get outside himself, who knows others only in himself, and when he says the contrary he lies." Maybe I have been honest in the poems I have written, and I have not lied by saying the contrary. Whether I have tried to get outside of myself is a matter of debate. But in my nature is my fate; for I have merely tried whenever possible to follow my own instincts and so discover in my own singular mind the features of other minds. A year back, on one of my visits to the tribal hinterland of Orissa. I spent a little time at a village called Barakamura deep in the forests of Similipal. My aimless wandering took me to a hilly stream where a woman was bathing with her son, a three-year-old. Uncertainty struck her withering face as I approached; she would be twenty-five but appeared to be fifty-five. I was curious. With trepidation I asked her, "What have you cooked to go with your rice today?" She was uneasy. The sadness of the world was recorded on her face. She said, "Rice? Where can we have rice, Babu?" My silence began to feed on her unending hardship. She added, "When some big Babu comes here, we have the good fortune to have rice, maybe once in two or three months. Or else it's whatever we can scrape off the forest."

It was only instinctive that I would use this incident in my poetry. In a way we are all participating in the catastrophies of the world; the enemy is always there, huge in his inhumanity, and any sensitive person sees him in the valleys of Kashmir, in the napalm-ridden girl running for her life in Vietnam, in the boy run over by a tank in Tiananmen Square, or at the World Trade Center in New York. As a feeling-being I cannot escape these wreckages of history, of my own past, like the inhuman and useless massacre of a hundred thousand Oriyas by the emperor Asoka in 261 B.C. I don't know if it is right to write about such things, because of the danger of the "glamour" a catastrophy carries with it. Maybe one is lying to oneself when one writes on a historical or political event. Maybe one is doing something similar to exploitation, gorging oneself on other people's suffering. Above everything else, poetry shouldn't make us lie. And yet, I have gone on to write on the starvation deaths in Kasipur in Orissa in the last month.

I have spoken a lot about myself, I realise. I shouldn't be doing this; for talking isn't the role of a poet. I still want to go on communicating through poetry with my readers. About twelve years back I suddenly discovered that all my supposed eloquence in English poetry had me drifting away from my own people. I was an outsider because I wrote in English, not Oriya. I made up my mind and earnestly began writing my poems in Oriya. Whether these Oriya poems reveal only my ineffectualness is a different matter. Whether some of my erudite readers sense a slight disgust in the poetry I write in Oriya doesn't oppress me much. Frankly, I felt excited at this new beginning of mine. I could talk now to the man in the street, to the newspaper boy, to the postman, through the new language. I used simple, colloquial words because my vocabulary in Oriya is severely limited. But I spoke with a literal nakedness. These poems did not have the sophistication of my English ones. They were different, complementary.

Maybe these were poems which revealed the naked truth in naked language, stripped of all exggerated aestheticism, I cannot say.

But my writing in Oriya was a blow in self-defence.

I had dropped my masks.

34

Slow Swim in Dim Light: The Quest for Modernity in Poetry

When I first started writing poetry and had already amassed a good number of poems on stray sheets of paper and in antiquated diaries, I decided to test my powers at poetry by sending the poems out to various periodicals. At that time, frankly, I knew very little about poetry, my knowledge of the subject being limited to the few poems of Keats, Shelley and Wordsworth that had been incorporated into our school literature texts. To me, this was a severe test; because the act of writing a poem was totally unknown to me. Added to this were two significant factors that went against my writing: first, I was old enough not to be getting ideas about those mushy qualities generally associated with a subject like love which almost all poets begin with; and secondly, I had been trained in a scientific discipline and been immersed in the teaching of Physics for a long time. Physics excited my senses, and I loved teaching it. So here I was, at a sort of crossroads, facing an impossible problem in my life.

At that time I was fast reaching the speculative age of forty—an age when my friends and colleagues smiled at me condescendingly when I admitted my aspirations before them. Were my poems mere games and diversions, I asked myself? I saw the unmistakable leer in their eyes, and felt fairly miserable. For me, certainly poetry was not the plaything they thought I was dabbling with. It was real for me, very real.

It became such a time when time itself could only silence the poetry I was beginning to write. But as I said earlier, if it became an impossible problem for me, the problem itself brought out possibilities that were more poetical than before.

So, those early poems I wrote were submitted by me to different journals, to some magazines whose names I had picked up by hearsay, and to others I discovered in the reading room of the college where I taught. It was like threading into the unknown, as intriguing an act as the writing of my own poems was perhaps. But there was a thrill, an exhilaration in the whole venture.

Rejections were much more numerous than the few acceptances of the poems which came my way. With no basic knowledge of making a poem, my efforts were in all probability directed toward something new, a 'modernity' in my poetry. Undeniably I did want to write poems that would be different from those that still stuck to my mind from my school days. On the other hand, my ideas of what would be called 'modern' in the realm of poetry were vague. Nor did I have any access to contemporary poetry then. The only thing I felt that stood in my favour was my strong stand on language—a language I had been scrupulously nurturing and polishing through the years, and which was something of an obsession with me. I loved the words, and moved with the twists and turns of the sounds, rejoicing in the profound shades of meaning that seemed to come from somewhere beyond the words themselves. Maybe it was only this fascination for the language that urged me on. So, when with some degree of indiscrimination and stupid boldness, I began to *make* a poem which read:

> Swans sink wordlessly to the carpet
> miles of polished floors
> reach out
> for the glass of voices
>
> There are gulls crying everywhere
> and glazed green grass
> in the park with the swans
> folding their cold throats

and titled it "I Hear My Fingers Sadly Touching an Ivory Key", I never realised the implications of what I was doing. Was this poetry, I asked myself again and again? Maybe it was not. But the mind does crave new modes of expression. And I found mine breaking free with an abandon I found hard to hold back.

Whether the outcome of such poems turned out to be meaningful, is another matter. But there was this resistance from critics here in India, although the said poem was accepted for publication and subsequently published in *Chicago Review*.

The fact remains that I was trying to create differently. Doesn't the imagination help to carry meaning? Maybe my study of Physics had come to polarise my thinking, it is difficult to say. But there was this need to invent my own legends, my very own rites of living and death.

The feeling that this poetry was different from what was being written here at that time was strengthened by letters of rejection from established poets and editors. I should like to quote from one such letter. It said:

> I am sorry I am unable to use your poems. There is an unmistakable poetic quality in almost all the poems, but something eludes me. I should like to understand what I want my readers to understand.

The last line of the letter ate into me. For, above all, it demonstrated that secure, recognised editors were not prepared to accept any change that went against the rules of an established formalism. To me, it seemed (and still seems) a thoroughly bourgeois statement. Admitting that I was using free form, and that the laxity of its use did lead to certain excesses in the poem, this did not call for such a dismissal. So the question: does the idea of modernity not envisage a change from the accepted mode, a sort of pragmatic deviation? And if this change exists, then it paves the way to a certain modernity in poetry.

One may or may not agree with this idea. Any aesthetic judgement is one of preference, a preference influenced by education, upbringing, attitudes and opinions often having little to do with art or aesthetics. And often these beliefs are irrationally based on factors—social or economic—factors which are determined by chance or chosen by the reader or critic himself as profitable to his career.

So, without any abstract objective standards as to what constitutes a good poem (or good art, in general), subjective factors often assume the utmost importance. The reader or critic is the passive result of his or her upbringing. It can therefore be assumed that the notion of any aesthetic rationale in art or literature does not hold good, so that no such judgement of intrinsic value or distinction is possible. Thus we are left with the judgement of the available literary market, which is truly questionable. To argue for durability as the ultimate test does not get around the problem, since 'immortality' is a mutable thing, as subject to the whims of posterity just as current work is to current whims. So the critic is subjective; but does that curtail the writer's judgement? One would say: So what? A writer does have the power, does have his or her moral right to shape in part his or her own destiny!

I began this essay by speaking about my own poems and the responses they evoked from various sources. The decision to work my own way (and my own reality) was exploratory. If the poems were curiosities, they represented the modernity I was trying to cope with. But were these forays truly a movement into modernism? It is not easy to answer this question myself. Undoubtedly in the background was the discipline of science and investigation; yet, there always persisted the idea of the self, which served as the main reference point in my poetry.

But the self is wrapped up in too many ambiguities for comfort. It was apparent to me that I was not writing the kind of poems in which meaning was stated clearly, explicitly; and that this poetry did not have a sharp focus was what the critic had in mind when he commented on my work. In other words, this poetry had no flat statements. What I was perhaps trying to do was to put together images and symbols so that the reader would draw the implicit connections for himself. Maybe in such poetry, context is all-important. For here only certain meanings of parts of the poem emerge to the exclusion of others. It could be that this approach to the writing of poetry goes to make the poem mysterious, even obscure—and I must admit here that obscurity has been a label applied to much of my work. However, one feels that if this type of poem has an appeal, then it does contain the seeds of the poem's own interpretation.

If this sort of poetry is difficult to handle, different as it is from accepted modes, resisting classification, what would be more suitable for it than to put it under 'modernity'? And examples of this modernity (first propounded by Pound and Eliot) in the writings of contemporary Indian poets are easily found. Such poems reveal how the apparently unconnected parts of these can focus on some intelligible meaning. One can reason reliably well that the poetry of the present day is no more difficult than that of the poets writing at the beginning of the century. But it *is* difficult in the sense that its understanding or coherence comes from a perfectly intelligible literary ideology, not from the sympathetic magic in the poem itself.

When one looks for the kind of coherence that is generated by the arrangement of a particular poem, rather than a coherence existing outside the poem, one finds understanding this sort of poem difficult. Here, for instance, is a poem "Smile and Smile" by Bal Sitaram Mardhekar, as translated from the Marathi by Sudhakar Marathe:

> The night is punctured by lamps,
> But someone pumps on still
> The darkness.
>
> Although maddened by laughing gas,
> Tears follow barks of weeping
> In tune.
>
> The rubbery night sat flat with a thud,
> But there's no spare tyre at all
> In space.
>
> Dogs keep licking on and on
> Leathery chicken-skin minds
> On a heap.
>
> Everyone who can, who can,
> Should bear the pall of
> The night.
>
> And pull the wool over the eyes
> A little, a little, but with
> A smile.
>
> Like the growling rubber dogs
> Grr, grr in the punctured
> Rubbery night!

Setting aside the fact that it is a translation, we find that a number of questions come to the mind when we read the poem. These are questions which we cannot answer, at least some of them. But a little thinking helps, and the poem becomes fairly clear in meaning when one considers it in the context of other poems like it, because of our familiarity with a shared contemporary language.

And the poem becomes an example of modernity. For, in this particular poem, we can ask ourselves questions like "Why should someone pump on still the darkness?" Or "Why maddened by 'laughing gas'?" Or "in tune?" Or why does the poem speak of "growling rubber dogs" at the end?

Certainly these are difficult to answer to our satisfaction. But the poem takes us from the beauty and terror of the night into the depths of the psyche. Here the poet speaks of a world where the night will be what it is: "punctured, rubbery", and with "no spare tyre at all in space".

"Smile and Smile" tantalises as a poem; a failure is evident about human existence, about which the poet supposedly can do very little. And the reader too. But can our world be otherwise, we ask, when we read this brief and perceptive Mardhekar poem?

In the poet's quest for modernity, the poet, always seeking excitement, reveals his own portraits of man's inner depths, giving us the presence of shadowy forms through which life goes on. At times these forms startle with fearful clarity, at other times they do not, remain ambiguous. Nevertheless, the poet in his or her search through the making of the poem, comes face to face with some mysterious presence—a presence which could hold its sacred magic, and which is grounded somewhere within the self. And perhaps there is the breaking out of a voice, which feels its way, speaking to no one in particular; but, once, written down, creates a relationship with the reader, wanting to be something that has not been seen or felt before, something beautiful and unforgettable and unmistakably modern:

> Suddenly lost
> In the dazzle of the fading day
> You, my little bird.
> With whom have you left to blossom
> Some name for the nude girl's sleep?
> The paddy doesn't ripen this year.
> Only beneath your eyelids
> Is a roaring fire like a red wind.
> Only you would have known
> What the season is now,
> You, my little bird
> Does the conch still sound
> Across the seven seas?

Reading and re-reading this poem "Suddenly Lost" by the distinguished Assamese poet Nilmoni Phukan (rendered into

English by D.N. Bezbaruah), I would say that the poem (for me) speaks to a place of sanctity within the self. Even at the very beginning when the poet addresses the "little bird", one becomes painfully aware that he is describing the sacred space in the self, away from "the dazzle of the fading day". Soon, questions associated with contemporaneous life appear, questions which are totally unanswerable. And yet, behind this apparent paradox of the poem which frustrates our understanding, is a reality that is held up by ideas. I would say unhesitatingly that Phookan has used those three substances which are the basic building blocks of life: light, space and time. And as life would cease if any one of them were withdrawn from the world, this poem would lose its mystery and its magic if similar images or symbols were removed from it.

An inner mystery seems to be the essence of this poem, as with other poems which can be classified as modernistic being written today in the regional languages of the country. Still, modernity is a word which doesn't yield a simple, easy interpretation. But one would be right if one associates this new poetry with a poetry of mystification.

Perhaps the unintentional purpose behind modernity is to disorient us, to throw the mind into disarray. By this, I think, one does not deliberately pursue a sort of confusion; only that one has to recognise that our accustomed ways of making sense are no longer reliable, and that the world we are familiar with, is no more held by those limits we had traditionally ascribed to it. Above all, modernity represents the direction in our attempts to find new bearings amid an unrefutable uncertainty, new ways of understanding, and finally, judging our experience.

That the uncertainty of modern living is partially responsible for this unstable equilibrium cannot be disclaimed. When I discussed the making of the poem "I Hear My Fingers Sadly Touching an Ivory Key" earlier, I knew I was inventing images, images which came from my own experience and my own learning, but which now were on the way to creating a different experience. Perhaps these images in the poem (I shall call it "modern") did not communicate as subject-predicate sentences do. As I said, these images emerge from convoluted tremors which take place (or have already taken place) deep inside the writer's self.

Generally, however, it is difficult to break into these images in a modernist poem. It was Paul Celan who remarked that his poems were meant to be accepted as "concrete imagery, *not* as codes needing deciphering." Maybe Kafka has done similar things in his shorter prose pieces. And the work of such modernist masters makes one ask: Can't truth be abstracted from the images that make such a poem?

Ignorant as I am of the trends in poetry in India in the many regional languages, it would be imprudent of me to make generalisations about modernistic currents in the poetry. Perhaps only after 1947, after independence, one could discern any modernities in various art forms, modernities that could be specifically called coherent. It would only be right for me to talk about the languages I know. Trends in the arts are always related to culture; so when technology entered people's lives in India, especially in the urban areas, this led to a modernistic culture in society. It seemed to be the proper time for the arts to take up this strain. Poetry too, in tune with the times, reacting to well-established formal, ritualistic religion, reacting to the brutal indifference of capitalism to poverty, showed this in disillusionment and despair. An open mode of expression, social and sexual, was urged on by a new liberal culture. It would be easy to give examples of this poetry produced in India.

And yet, perhaps, poetry is the only art form which doesn't show all these trends in strength, in contrast to the experimental techniques utilised by the visual mass media or the rebellion voiced in the pop music culture of the young. For us, in Orissa, religion is still vital, and is a way of life; the danger that characterises urban civil societies seems to be absent. Where then is the *need* for such modernity in a society which has remained fundamentally static through the years? Where does this *need* for individualism come in, the individualism which is the seed of modernity? Or, for experiment and rebellion in the arts?

Bertolt Brecht once said that many artists tried to create works for the masses, not for a narrow elite. But this is a mistake, said Brecht. The real problem is not that we have to work for the masses; we must bring about that change from a narrow elite to a large elite. And with this in mind, without forsaking our cultural past, we should prepare best for the events of the future.

35

Mirror of a Mirror

Men have long memories. Each one of us, in a way, is "made" out of his or her own past—and that past, in essence, goes back to one's childhood. A trivial incident, an apparently innocuous word, or a gesture; these burrow their tunnels in the deep recesses of the child's mind, in turn becoming such "memories" which *lock* us inside our own selves—and eventually urge us to cope with the complexities of life in many different ways.

Today, I cannot seem to shake off the feeling that my childhood was an unhappy one. Yet, I remember, we seemed to have all the basic necessities of life—the daily meals, a house, both parents, and a discerning school in which I studied. Perhaps all these are the trappings of civilisation, and were really "extras"; because many children, most of them my neighbours, did not have enough to eat at that time, making me suffer from the thought that I was needlessly robbing them of their due. Nevertheless, the fact remains, I was unhappy. Almost left to myself for reasons I wouldn't like to talk here, there was no other recourse for me but to seek escape in the world of books. A somewhat sickly constitution added to my ordeal. Reading, therefore, took up much of my time; and I usually spent the lunch break even at school with some story book in the shade of the huge tamarind tree by the school pool.

Fiction, the reading of it, appeared to fascinate me, for here was the world of imagination made real, leading to the getaway I felt I needed from my immediate environment. However, my entire reading then was limited to English: and so it was that I began to discover newer and newer authors, already feeling excited by the quality of the language they used. And gradually, I revelled in these alien words, their sibilances and their moods, going on to imitate the language of the time—perhaps a foretaste of the joys of authorship.

It was then that I suddenly found myself at the boundary between two separate worlds, or that was what I thought at the time. With my aptitude for Physics and Mathematics, I embarked simultaneously upon the theories of evolution and the laws of exact sciences, which seemed to be in distinct contradiction with the island-faith of my childhood religion had forced upon me. I did not know where to turn; for even my father's eyes did appear empty of scientific knowledge. I looked into those familiar eyes of his but saw nothing there save the roots of a faith he *chose* to understand. Around me was sickness and hunger, the sufferings of people from malnutrition and disease—a terrible form of disorder of the universe that made me question myself on the goodness of God we had been taught to believe in. And so I felt unable to reconcile these two affirmations—that God is the sum of all perfection, and that the world of ours, with all its imperfections was created by Him.

It was around the year 1951 that I came across one of those books that made a profound impact on my life. Our college library was a veritable haven of sensible reading matter. I had just joined as a lecturer in Physics and was assigned to teach four classes a week. This left me enough time to pursue my own reading and explore the dust-filled shelves of the sprawling library. I had finished reading the saga of the Thibaults written by the French novelist Roger

Martin du Gard, and the character of Dr. Antoine Thibault made me go *into* myself, perhaps helping me to see myself better. Soon enough, I was fortunate to pick up another book by the same author from a bookshop near my college. It was titled *Jean Barois.* Here, confronting me, was the central character of the book, a young scientist called Jean Barois—very moral and upright, who went on to question himself and his actions, because of his inner need of personal integrity. I felt attracted to him at once, identifying myself with his thoughts and ideas. Here du Gard attacks the age-old theme of Reason versus Faith, portraying it at a time and in a setting where it presented itself with a peculiar vividness and intensity.

Today I still go back into the discoloured pages of the book I had bought with much thought and with the money of my meagre salary in mid-1951. Fifty years have gone by, but the words in the book still ring true. Jean Barois spoke then of the "lies, selfishness, injustice" which "flourish exactly as they did before." "Where then can you see progress?" he asks.

"Try as we may to bring freedom to our fellow-men and to better their lot, human nature is against us." Jean Barois breaks down when he utters this poignant sentence, and I have not been able to see otherwise, even as we near the end of the twentieth century. With each new generation all the old mistakes, the same injustices, rear their ugly heads; it's always the same dreary struggle, the same victory of the strong over the weak, of the young over the old.

It seems to me that in an indifferent world, man cannot rely either on nature or on his fellow human beings; but that he must be able to rely on himself and on those few friends who share the same feelings. Perhaps Jean Barois in *Jean Barois* has showed me *how to be true to myself,* more than any dogmatic teaching of religion can. A man is, as he is. I have tried all my life, by instinct rather than by deliberate choice, to be loyal to the commitments I have made, to the ones I love, and to my country. At times I have made mistakes when faced with contradictory loyalties. And with no small measure of anguish, I have learned to admit my wrongs and to submit and to live.

36

A. K. Ramanujan: A Tribute

The death of a poet, or writer, is seldom noticed or talked about. This is common knowledge, a fact which is accepted without question. There are no headlines announcing the poet's death; only a close reading of a newspaper may reveal pitifully a brief mention in an obscure corner in an inner page, perhaps pushed in beside some loud advertisement. And if the poet chooses to live, not in his land but away somewhere, then it is supposedly normal behaviour that not much coverage in the media be given to him.

A poet who could fit in with these observations was A.K. Ramanujan who died last July in the USA. I learnt of his death from an editorial piece in a daily newspaper; prior to this I had not come across any report of this sudden tragedy—a tragedy which concerned all lovers of literature. I thought this rather pathetic.

But maybe I am wrong. Deaths of friends, who more or less live and think as one does, only help to bring up one's world nearer; revealing an inner face which one had somehow not seen until that moment. The death of Ramanujan suddenly seemed to change something in my life; I began to remember things I had carelessly overlooked, making me want to say what I had not said for years.

The best way to talk about a poet is through his poems, and to my mind the best way to pay tribute to such a master of the brief word is to read his poems, as evident in this short poem titled "On the Death of a Poem":

Images consult
one
another,

a conscience-
stricken
jury,

and come
slowly
to a sentence.

Open out the words of this poem, and it is a single sentence. But what a marvellous one! Like an oriental box, a little difficult to open perhaps, but superbly beautiful. A poem that holds magic in its lines!

So this was a Ramanujan poem. Several personalities at once, he was scholar, folklorist, translator and bilingual poet, a rare example of the Brahminical virtue of learning. He will be remembered for the inquiry he brought into South Indian culture, sweeping, as it were, the ancient literature of India into the arena of the present day. And he did this with a rare sensitivity. If you read on carefully, you will notice his keen observations, and the drama of his own life, observed by his Upanishadic "watchers...from their nowhere perches." And yet, the irony he chose to portray in his poems was so naturally done, that one would not turn upon it.

A.K. Ramanujan was just 64 when he died. He was educated at Maharaja's College, Mysore; Deccan College, Pune and Indiana University. He taught at the University of Chicago from 1962 to 1993, a long period of over 30 years, primarily in the Department of South Asian Languages and Civilizations.

He was the author of more than 15 books. In his celebrated translations from the medieval Kannada and ancient Tamil literatures, *Speaking of Siva, The Interior Landscape, Poems of Love and War,* he illuminated the religious verses of the Kannada *bhakti* poets, and the highly stylised, imagistic stanzas of the Sangam anthologists who represent the fountainhead of Tamil literary culture. Moving between past and present, between his homes here in India and America, Ramanujan once said:

> It looks as if I live between things all the time—two (or more) languages, two countries, two disciplines. My translations are a way to keep them all together.

This plurality is best seen in his own poems: the wonderfully-crafted gems in his books, *The Striders*, *Relations* and *Second Sight*. He came back time and again to the themes of the family, and the "palimpsest of subcontinental history." Both as poet and translator, Ramanujan tried to keep open the dialogue between cultures.

More recently, he edited two books—one on Indian folklore, and the other on our literatures.

I had known Ramanujan for many years, long before I had started writing myself. I cannot deny now, that at one time in my life, I had tried to write like him. His was the predicament of the artist, the issue between involvement and a detachment of problems that concerned him.

But I would not end this without a brief reference to the man himself. Ramanujan was a true picture of gentleness, of humility itself. Four years ago, at an international festival of writers and scholars in West Germany, we met; our first ever meeting, also our last. How ironical that we were to meet in a neutral land. I say neutral because it was neither Ramanujan's homeland nor mine.

India seemed so far away then, as we spoke of things trivial, not the poetry we wrote. It was a meeting I will not easily forget. Little did I know this would be the last time I'd see him.

It was a rare gift for me—the day we spent talking at the scenic university town of Marburg—precious as all the work he chose to leave behind, like this poem titled "Anxiety":

> Not branchless as the fear tree,
> it has naked roots and sacred twigs.
> Not geometric as the parabolas
> of hope, it has loose ends

with a knot at the top
that's me.

Not wakeful in its white-snake
glassy ways like the cloping gaiety of waters,
it drowses, viscous and fibered as pitch.

Flames have only lungs. Water is all eyes.
The earth has bone for muscle. And the air
is a flock of invisible pigeons.
But anxiety
can find no metaphor to end it.

37

Time in the Poem

As I see it, the act of writing a poem is like being caught up in a net of time, in which the space of experience helps to guide the feeling contained in the poem. The poem becomes the precise moment of a truth, and that moment comes through a procession of events or thoughts which take place in the poet's mind. In the making of a poem a crowding together of events or beings occurs; this is what one discovers through the act itself, and we could call this a sort of charging of the usual neutral senses that inhabit the mind of the poet. This process acts equally strongly irrespective of the quality of the poem the poet is able to produce, whether bad or good. But it is time itself that makes the poet realise that he should react, a time that appears to pass from somewhere inside himself into the outer world, similar perhaps to the lines of force that emanate from an electrical charge situated in space (or from a magnetic pole). Yet in a strange manner the time of the present which brings forth his responses, has in reality come into being from the many times he has encountered— a product of memory. It is a reversible process, and seems to work both ways. So a time encompasses him, coming back to him as it were, and the poet is left in a net in his consciousness.

This might appear on the surface as a dilemma, a dilemma that stems from the irrefutable fact that time owns us, body and soul. Yet we are not absolute victims of time. Because each one of us finds himself responsible for what happens to us during our lives. The fundamental observation that a man or woman is born at a precise instant of time (fixed by a set of coordinates), makes him a certain prisoner, true; and this fact lives at the back of his head probably for an initial number of years of his life. It is later, perhaps much later, for the not-so-sensitive, that time begins to bother them. Therefore, in a way, time becomes the main mover of our lives. And in the making of a poem, it is not the ordinary, run-of-the-mill type of being, who as indications show, turns out to be a practising poet—but an acute, feeling and more aware being. The awareness of this poet may be exceptional, making him/her a hypersensitive person, or a suicidal depressive; leading the person to such an extraordinary degree of stimulation that he/she writes the kind of poem he/she feels in the unconscious.

It is this aspect of time that has led me into my poems, and it makes me feel that most poets go about their poems in the same way. As I start the poem with a particular instant of time I am aware that the instant has ceased to *be* once I have put the feeling down; or precisely speaking, that which constituted the line(s) of the poem. And as the poem proceeds, with the series of images helping to build up the matter of the poem, I realise with some measure of emotion, that the time of the poem is no more with me, and this is what has made the poem non-existent. In other words, it has lost its original identity. It becomes a human dilemma in the sense that the poem, once written down, ceases to dominate the poet's consciousness; and this is what is significant to me as a poet, that the poem no longer has the voice I tried to imbibe into it, but presents another face—a face which is seen or determined by the reader of the poem, a reader who, once again, is held by a totally different instant of time.

It is difficult for me to infer that other practitioners of poetry share my view, i.e., the poem is left behind in another time as the new present begins to weigh one down with its weight. This happens primarily because the writing of poems is a continuous activity, and when a poem gets over, it is time which once again does not spare the poet's mind but "poisons" it with the restlessness of movement, something resembling the constant random motion of subatomic particles inside the nucleus of an atom. That such a mood keeps on nagging me until I go over to the making of another poem is a truth, even if the next one only helps me to escape the pursuing push of time by writing, perhaps merely to fill up a page with common stuff. Thus, between one poem and the next, the mind becomes an indiscipline of reactions. This multiple activity occupies the poet, measuring him by a constantly moving point of time that finally turns into a poem, whether trivial or significant; and it is this knowledge of the essence of time which unconsciously becomes the poet's rationalism.

If I go back and ask myself the unnecessary question as to why I started writing poetry, at a time when most other poets would have produced more or less their best work, perhaps the overwhelming sense of the inevitability of ageing was the main drive behind my writing. It was the common enough feeling of loss of years of my life, coupled with a space of isolation, that represented the "crisis" which ultimately goaded me to write. For who can deny that it is such a crisis that is the source of poetry? To my mind, in the last years of his life, Robert Penn Warren had been producing some of the best poetry in the United States, and this too when he had already reached the advanced age of seventy-five. His poems about time, centering on the possible clairvoyance in death, keep looking out over our lives. And one feels certain that it is time which almost always brings out the meditative weight in his later poems.

So, perhaps my very own first poem in my first book, titled "Loneliness"—a mediocre poem by any standards, but still meaningful to me because it answers in some ways the question of my writing, the 'why'. And because this first book was published in the autumn of 1971, when I was forty-three, is this presence of time in the entrails of that poem, admitted that the poem itself is a bad example of verse.

A poem, therefore, appears to me to be full or made up of various times, maybe like a dim corner in a room, inhabited by a number of spiders. Even though the poem generally is set around a certain event which takes place at a particular moment of time; even though one is speaking of, say, the death of a boy, or the ending of another year, or, about the shapes that inhabit the river Daya—it is time which becomes an eight-legged carnivorous spider weaving its ensnaring net in which the poem is trapped. To be more precise in my statement, it is the underlying emotional force of the poem that is trapped. Perhaps in the process of making the poem it is nostalgia which plays a significant part, as many moments, past and present, build their nets across their words and wait for the outcome.

On the surface, the poem may emerge as a result of the summation of events or happenings at a number of times. In other words, the poem $= \Sigma (et_1 + et_2 + et_3 + ...)$, where t_1, t_2, t_3...represent different instants of time when the emotional forces in the poem came into play. And yet, such a generalisation could be full of error. This is because a poem does not represent an algebraic summation of emotional operatives. The conclusion or outcome of a good or successful poem will only happen, when, mathematically speaking, the summation is replaced by an integral, the integration taking place over the entire time in which the poem works. So perhaps the poem $= \int_{T_1}^{T_2} e = \int_{t_1}^{t_1+\partial t_1} e + \int_{t_2}^{t_2+\partial t_2} e + \int_{t_3}^{t_3+\partial t_3} e + ...$, where the symbols have their usual significance. Every item in the poem is fixed and accessible. The poet can only integrate the entire process according to his or her own capacity. And the poet makes the poem *move.*

So to write his poem, the poet will be obliged to turn inward, decelerating, as he seeks out the time as it exists in him. Because the poem is a parasite around that moment which the poet perceives and which takes him into the making of the poem. Hardly has the moment entered the mind or the consciousness of their poet when it becomes caught in a mesh of other moments of time. These moments move back and forth in the poet's mind sweeping through all the years of his lifetime. At times time rushes toward him, a terrifying cataclysm, until he and his poem are drowned in the sweeping flood. I don't think the poet will have anywhere to run then. I don't think the poet would've stopped short of the horizon, his longest memory. Because time has him trapped between his memories and the moments of his own consciousness.

I'd like to give an example of such a poem, enmeshed in time, titled "The Hour Before Dawn", first published in *The Hudson Review:*

> It was the hour before dawn. I awoke.
> The street lamp stared lamely at my window
> and a world was quiet, bewildered
> as though afraid it would be lost
> among thoughts. I waited for a sound,
> a rain to fall and tear this silence
> between today and tomorrow.
> On a distant tree a light breeze combed

the leaves of darkness without a whisper.
And through the window peered my love and fear
and dreams that were mere dummies to the hour.
Unknowing, I bring my palms together.
I remember the one I loved once,
but she seemed to have another face.
My father, sad-faced father! How very far you are
from this empty room filled only with myself!
Without a sound the dark tree out there
struggles with its death in my life.
The silent world floats besides me;
tomorrow may be I'll hear my father is dead,
but he might bear the face of my son.
This is the hour when there is no distance
between the two of them.
The hour of awakening, when my speechless voice
echoes only from my father to my son,
coming to rest on the lamp post
like a weary night bird.

So this poem, which does not show the time of one single instant. But which begins from an instant, an instant inside an experience and goes on to measure spiritual and physical dimensions from other instants associated with it.

We are all playing with time, all the while, though we do not realise this. This sounds like a cliche. Yet, in a poem, more than any other form of literature, prose or whatever, one is taking up time in one's hands, shortening it, lengthening it—playing with it in a manner that is not possible as much as in any other literary form. Maybe it is like a mass of putty in the fingers of our mind, while we wait for an identifiable shape to emerge. And this maelstrom of time is held in the unconscious, into which dawns and sunsets, and time from every conceivable instant, from past, present and future, bring up their objects. Here the poem shows its real self, threading different phenomena from many instants of time.

In a way, the poem is caught. Would it be wrong, I wonder, if I said that the time of the poem is caught like a patient in a mental asylum, between the states of her mind? Time here moves back and forth between memory and possibility, becoming an obsession of the present. Therefore, it is a state the poem never leaves. The present is a moment the poet perceives, employing his poem around that moment, realising fully well that his 'moment' is an infinite oscillation in time.

With almost four or five thousand years of poetry behind us in India, with one's roots in an ancient mass of myth and legend, one cannot help being permeated by their time. It is time which forms the worn stone and the brown earth on which we exist, time that induces in us a blueness of the sky that is indeed differently blue from the normal blue we know of and has come to stay from the writings of others. A blue that makes up the wisdom of poetry. So with a kind of anguish the poem begins to form on paper, as though the human mind whirled with unchanging rites of time, and then got transfixed in itself.

In the beginning, writing a poem for any poet is an act which ends in an upsurge of joy, of something achieved, perhaps irrespective of whether the poem was a good one or bad. But with the passing of years, one comes to realise that the fabric of the envelope which stretches taut over the framework of the years is made out of time. In my own case, ill health has been an added hazard, hastening the making of my poetry. Maybe as far as I could, I have salvaged the hours of loss for my own self-expression in poetry. Or, is the poem a safety measure, a strategic reserve in case time plotted a crisis in my life and I needed a way out? And the poem is not a cry.

It is an abrupt opening of the eyelids as it functions in time, as time balances itself on the tightrope of memories.

And as a practising poet, I feel time acts as a carrier wave, acting between question and response, and doing the work in the poem. Perhaps, as one comes to the end of the poem, one sees some sense in the statement that the language of poetry is made up of time, not words. This is because, very simply, when I look back on a poem written a long time ago, I can see my very existence at the moment the poem was made, carrying me away on the tide of the poem's nostalgia. And this feeling can have a disastrous effect on the new poem I am trying to write.

Today I dream. So I sit down to write. I feel the confusing waves of time's pain so much so, that at times I would like to use time as an avenging god in my poem. At other moments, or in between poems, time is just a frail ghost of an enemy standing ahead in my path, and when I sense I could go through it, unscathed. And as I advance, both in my poetry and in my years, I feel I am perhaps driving the victim of time ahead of me.